OPPOSING
VIEWPOINTS®
SERIES

Teen Dating

Other Books of Related Interest

Opposing Viewpoints Series

Street Teens
Student Life
Teenage Sexuality
Teens at Risk

At Issue Series

Sexting
Teen Driving
Teen Sex
Teens and Credit

Current Controversies Series

Teen Pregnancy and Parenting
Teens and Privacy

"Congress shall make
no law ... abridging
the freedom of speech,
or of the press."

First Amendment to the US Constitution

The basic foundation of our democracy is the First Amendment guarantee of freedom of expression. The Opposing Viewpoints Series is dedicated to the concept of this basic freedom and the idea that it is more important to practice it than to enshrine it.

OPPOSING
VIEWPOINTS®
SERIES

Teen Dating

Louise I. Gerdes, Book Editor

GREENHAVEN PRESS
A part of Gale, Cengage Learning

GALE
CENGAGE Learning·

Detroit • New York • San Francisco • New Haven, Conn • Waterville, Maine • London

Elizabeth Des Chenes, *Director, Publishing Solutions*

© 2013 Greenhaven Press, a part of Gale, Cengage Learning

Gale and Greenhaven Press are registered trademarks used herein under license.

For more information, contact:
Greenhaven Press
27500 Drake Rd.
Farmington Hills, MI 48331-3535
Or you can visit our Internet site at gale.cengage.com.

For product information and technology assistance, contact us at:

Gale Customer Support, 1-800-877-4253.
For permission to use material from this text or product, submit all requests online at www.cengage.com/permissions.

Further permissions questions can be emailed to permissionrequest@cengage.com.

Articles in Greenhaven Press anthologies are often edited for length to meet page requirements. In addition, original titles of these works are changed to clearly present the main thesis and to explicitly indicate the author's opinion. Every effort is made to ensure that Greenhaven Press accurately reflects the original intent of the authors. Every effort has been made to trace the owners of copyrighted material.

Cover image © Dayna More/Shutterstock.com.

LIBRARY OF CONGRESS CATALOGING-IN-PUBLICATION DATA

Teen dating / Louise I. Gerdes, book editor.
    p. cm. -- (Opposing viewpoints)
  Includes bibliographical references and index.
  ISBN 978-0-7377-6344-7 (hbk.) -- ISBN 978-0-7377-6345-4 (pbk.)
1. Dating violence. 2. Dating (Social customs) 3. Teenagers--Social life and customs. 4. Teenagers--Sexual behavior. I. Gerdes, Louise I., 1953-
  HQ801.83.T44 2013
  306.73--dc23

                                    2012033955

Printed in the United States of America
1 2 3 4 5   17 16 15 14 13

Contents

Chapter 3: What Impact Do Media and Technology Have on Teen Dating?

Why Consider
Opposing Viewpoints?

*"The only way in which a human being
can make some approach to knowing
the whole of a subject is by hearing
what can be said about it by persons of
every variety of opinion and studying
all modes in which it can be looked at
by every character of mind. No wise
man ever acquired his wisdom in any
mode but this."*

John Stuart Mill

In our media-intensive culture it is not difficult to find differing opinions. Thousands of newspapers and magazines and dozens of radio and television talk shows resound with differing points of view. The difficulty lies in deciding which opinion to agree with and which "experts" seem the most credible. The more inundated we become with differing opinions and claims, the more essential it is to hone critical reading and thinking skills to evaluate these ideas. Opposing Viewpoints books address this problem directly by presenting stimulating debates that can be used to enhance and teach these skills. The varied opinions contained in each book examine many different aspects of a single issue. While examining these conveniently edited opposing views, readers can develop critical thinking skills such as the ability to compare and contrast authors' credibility, facts, argumentation styles, use of persuasive techniques, and other stylistic tools. In short, the Opposing Viewpoints Series is an ideal way to attain the higher-level thinking and reading skills so essential in a culture of diverse and contradictory opinions.

In addition to providing a tool for critical thinking, Opposing Viewpoints books challenge readers to question their own strongly held opinions and assumptions. Most people form their opinions on the basis of upbringing, peer pressure, and personal, cultural, or professional bias. By reading carefully balanced opposing views, readers must directly confront new ideas as well as the opinions of those with whom they disagree. This is not to argue simplistically that everyone who reads opposing views will—or should—change his or her opinion. Instead, the series enhances readers' understanding of their own views by encouraging confrontation with opposing ideas. Careful examination of others' views can lead to the readers' understanding of the logical inconsistencies in their own opinions, perspective on why they hold an opinion, and the consideration of the possibility that their opinion requires further evaluation.

Evaluating Other Opinions

To ensure that this type of examination occurs, Opposing Viewpoints books present all types of opinions. Prominent spokespeople on different sides of each issue as well as well-known professionals from many disciplines challenge the reader. An additional goal of the series is to provide a forum for other, less known, or even unpopular viewpoints. The opinion of an ordinary person who has had to make the decision to cut off life support from a terminally ill relative, for example, may be just as valuable and provide just as much insight as a medical ethicist's professional opinion. The editors have two additional purposes in including these less known views. One, the editors encourage readers to respect others' opinions—even when not enhanced by professional credibility. It is only by reading or listening to and objectively evaluating others' ideas that one can determine whether they are worthy of consideration. Two, the inclusion of such viewpoints encourages the important critical thinking skill of objectively evaluating an author's credentials and bias. This evaluation will illuminate an author's reasons for taking a particular stance on an issue and will aid in readers' evaluation of the author's ideas.

It is our hope that these books will give readers a deeper understanding of the issues debated and an appreciation of the complexity of even seemingly simple issues when good and honest people disagree. This awareness is particularly important in a democratic society such as ours in which people enter into public debate to determine the common good. Those with whom one disagrees should not be regarded as enemies but rather as people whose views deserve careful examination and may shed light on one's own.

Thomas Jefferson once said that "difference of opinion leads to inquiry, and inquiry to truth." Jefferson, a broadly educated man, argued that "if a nation expects to be ignorant and free . . . it expects what never was and never will be." As individuals and as a nation, it is imperative that we consider the opinions of others and examine them with skill and discernment. The Opposing Viewpoints Series is intended to help readers achieve this goal.

David L. Bender and Bruno Leone,
Founders

Introduction

Most agree that the word *teen* emerged during World War II to describe children who had not entered the workforce and were often still living at home. Before the term emerged, people were most often described as either children or adults. The entry into adulthood, although determined to some degree by age, also was established by social guidelines such as marriage for girls and by entry into the workforce for boys, although this varied among the different classes. However, several economic and social changes early in the twentieth century created a new demographic group, and the word *teen* emerged to describe children between the ages of twelve and twenty. Child labor laws removed poor children from hard labor and kept them in school. In addition, economic conditions and social reforms encouraged parents from all social classes to keep their children in school for longer periods. Moreover, while a college education was once available only to the privileged, changing social attitudes and policies made it possible for the children of middle- and even working-class families to go on to college. This delayed the entrance into the adult workforce for more and more children in their teens.

Although social pressures continued to control how people met and married, economic and social changes in the first half of the twentieth century also contributed to the development of the practice of dating. Because children stayed in school longer, they also delayed the age of marriage. Even before the twentieth century began, fewer people were marrying for economic reasons or to meet social obligations. Thus, women and men were to a greater extent free to choose their marriage partners. Thus, a need to get to know potential marriage partners was necessary. Although dating—the courtship of potential romantic partners to assess their suitability—began earlier in the twentieth century, the teen dating process most are familiar with today emerged following World War II at the same time that more people began to see teens as a separate demographic group. In the early years, dating among teens was closely monitored by parents. However, as personal and family income grew, many teens were able to buy cars or at the very least use the family car. Access to automobiles, combined with other cultural developments that created special meeting places that appealed mostly to youth, created greater privacy for dating teens, making parental monitoring more difficult. In the eyes of some, this lack of monitoring contributed to the first teen dating concern to gain public attention—teen pregnancy.

When teen pregnancy reached its peak in 1957—96.3 births per 1,000—what had once been a family problem that was addressed privately—unmarried pregnancy—became a public health issue. That teens would engage in premarital sex was no surprise for many social scientists who define adolescence as a period of mental and physical development when children begin to take on adult characteristics, particularly sexual characteristics and behaviors. Thus, while some believed that because teens stayed in school for longer periods and deferred marriage they would also suppress their sexual development, other social scientists suggested that many teens would not be able to meet the challenge. Indeed, the reality became quickly apparent in 1957, as did the perception that dating teens had special concerns that warranted special attention. Competing progressive and socially conservative values about what policies would best address the teen pregnancy problem would also frame teen dating policy debates that grew from these early concerns. Although juvenile crime had been a hotly contested debate following World War II, teen pregnancy was the first teen dating issue to garner sizeable public attention. In the decades that followed, other social concerns such as domestic violence and the impact of the media and technology would lead to related teen dating concerns. Warring values would also color these teen dating policy debates. In fact, such conflicting attitudes are clearly visible in the debate over whether casual oral sex and oral sex parties, often called "hook-ups" and "rainbow parties," are a disturbing trend or what others call problem inflation.

One of the first reports of a teen oral sex problem followed a July 1998 scandal in Arlington, Virginia, in which a group of eighth-graders reportedly gathered at parties to be paired off for petting and ultimately oral sex. The story appeared on the front page of the *Washington Post*, bearing the headline, "Parents Are Alarmed by an Unsettling New Fad in Middle Schools: Oral Sex." The incident was soon generalized by media and both progressive and social conservative public policy advocates to a broader population of teens, although the evidence was anecdotal. Claims that casual oral sex was now common among teens increased in fervor following a 2003 episode of the *Oprah Winfrey Show* in which *O* magazine editor Michelle Burford revealed that "rainbow parties" were common. According to interviews, girls wearing different colors of lipstick would take turns performing oral sex on several boys so that the boys would have a rainbow of colors on their penises. No evidence was ever provided that the girls interviewed had actually participated. In fact, reports of rainbow parties have never been substantiated. Nevertheless, fears persist. Writer Caitlin Flanagan maintains, "The moms in my set are convinced—they're certain; they know for a *fact*—that all over the city, in the very best schools, in the nicest families, in the leafiest neighborhoods, twelve- and thirteen-year-old girls are performing oral sex on as many boys as they can . . . on school buses, and in bathrooms, libraries, and stairwells. They're making bar mitzvah presents of the act."[1]

The conservative Kaiser Family Foundation did, in fact, find that one-third of teens surveyed had engaged in oral sex. Later surveys would reveal even higher numbers. Interviews with teens also appear to support the phenomenon. "Every girl in this school has given head. A lot of girls think it's icky, but they do it anyway to get the boys' attention,"[2] explained one Washington, DC, teen. In addition to social conservatives, analysts with other perspectives and motives fear rising teen oral sex statistics, but for different reasons. For example, while social conservatives find any form of premarital sex morally unacceptable, some social scientists fear that increasing reports of casual oral sex among teens will make it difficult to form healthy relationships. Wisconsin sociologist Marline Pearson believes, "There is more and more sex without meaning."[3] She explains that "it's going to be hard for girls, who tend to expect sex to be something more than physical release."[4] Pearson maintains that most girls want sex to be meaningful, but with casual oral sex "girls are getting stuck with the lowest level of male sexuality: casual sex and blow-jobs." Many feminists agree. They argue that boys are often the recipients of oral sex and girls do so only to please them while at the same time avoiding the risks of vaginal intercourse. They conclude that oral sex thus entitles boys and disempowers girls.

Advocates representing progressive values use statistics about teen oral sex to promote comprehensive sex education, which they claim will reduce teen pregnancy and sexually transmitted disease, and reject abstinence-only education programs. They suggest that abstinence-only programs foster the idea that oral sex is an effective substitute for intercourse, thus contributing to higher oral sex numbers. In truth, Claire Brindis, pediatrics professor at the University of California at San Francisco, believes that teens have in fact weighed the advantages and dis-advantages of intercourse over other forms of sex and find that the risks of intercourse—pregnancy and sexually transmitted illnesses—are greater. However, she fears, "they may not have been given a strong enough message about the risks of oral sex. Maybe we need to do a better job of showing them they need to use condoms."[5]

Still others deny the existence of a teen oral sex epidemic altogether, claiming that it is a media-driven moral panic that appeals to parents' fears as their children are educated in increas-ingly culturally diverse environments. In fact, a 2008 Guttmacher Institute survey indicated that teens are not substituting oral for vaginal sex nor are they having casual oral sex with multiple part-ners. Columbia University sociology professor Peter Bearman is firm in his belief that casual oral sex "hookups" are an imagined problem. Bearman worked with researchers in the federal gov-ernment's National Longitudinal Study of Adolescent Health, which followed ninety thousand adolescents for more than ten years. He claims that the teen oral sex epidemic is a "made-up fantasy of white middle-class mothers whose kids are in diverse environments."[6] Indeed, according to Laura Sessions Stepp, au-thor of *Unhooked: How Young Women Pursue Sex, Delay Love, and Lose at Both*, "We're afraid to believe it about our own kids, but we're eager to believe it about other kids." Thus, the author ex-plains, "if our own kid does it, we can believe it's peer pressure."[7]

Others assert that parental fears surrounding oral or any other form of teen sex are more complex. Sarah Brown of the National Campaign to Prevent Teen Pregnancy believes that while oral sex is in fact infrequent, it does occur, and parents are confused because "the intimacy sequence has been turned on its head."[8] When the parents of teens today were coming of age, oral sex was the last sexual practice they would engage in, some not even until they were married. Today, among some teens, it is the first sexual practice they perform. Thus, what some parents think of as the most intimate sexual practice has become the least.

Accordingly, in the eyes of some commentators, parents' fears are stoked by stories of oral sex parties and hookups as they feel unprepared to deal with new sexual attitudes. Art and culture commentator Jennie Yabroff suggests that some parents believe salacious stories about teens, "possibly because they confirm parents' sense that they really have no idea what's going on with their kids. Or maybe it's easier to pay attention to a few shocking anecdotes than what the data—or our children—tell us."[9] Yabroff also asserts that adult misperceptions may also be due to the fact that the language of teen sexuality is unclear. "When an adolescent talks about hooking up, she may be describing a range of activities form kissing to intercourse."[10]

Still others who believe claims of a teen oral sex epidemic are unfounded assert that rainbow parties are simply urban legend. In fact, teens trained to discuss sex with peers in the Bronx and on the Lower East Side in New York City reported that they had never heard of rainbow parties, although they did hear teens speak about oral sex. Health professionals also report a similar lack of evidence of oral sex parties. "There was a posting on the Society for Adolescent Medicine listserv, asking if anyone had heard about rainbow parties, and no one knew anything about them,"[11] said Dr. Donna Futterman, a clinical pediatrics professor. Indeed, finding trustworthy data on teen sex is a challenge, and some social scientists claim that no clear picture of a potential casual oral sex problem is possible because reliable research is difficult to obtain. According to Bill Albert, chief program officer of the National Campaign to Prevent Teen Pregnancy, "parents of 13-year-olds don't want strangers asking their children questions about oral sex."[12]

In truth, public fears of a teen oral sex epidemic, whether real or imagined, have over the years since that first *Washington Post* headline come, gone, and reemerged, only to fade again. Researchers continue to compile statistics on teen sexual behavior, and surveys do in fact reveal that the number of teens engaging in oral sex is growing. Reliable information on whether these encounters are intimate or casual is more difficult to come by. Nevertheless, some consider oral sex among teens a problem worthy of public concern, and the policies that will best help dating teens remain hotly contested. The tension between those who debate these policies and those who believe that the reported teen oral sex epidemic is simply an unwarranted moral panic is reflected in *Opposing Viewpoints: Teen Dating* in the following chapters: Is Teen Dating Violence a Serious Problem?, What Issues Surround Teen Sex?, and What Impact Do Media and Technology Have on Teen Dating? How policy makers will manage the problems teens encounter in the face of public panic over teen behavior remains to be seen. *New York Times* columnist David Brooks is optimistic about America's youth:

> You could get the impression that America's young people are leading lives of Caligulan hedonism. You could give credence to all those parental scare stories about oral sex parties at bar mitzvahs and junior high school dances. You could worry about hookups, friends with benefits, and the rampant spread of casual, transactional sexuality. But it turns out you'd be wrong.[13]

Notes

1. Caitlin Flanagan, "Are You There God? It's Me Monica," *Atlantic*, January–February 2006.
2. Quoted in Jane Friedman, "Teen Sex," *CQ Researcher*, September 16, 2005.
3. Quoted in Friedman, "Teen Sex."
4. Quoted in Friedman, "Teen Sex."
5. Laura Sessions Stepp, "Study: Half of All Teens Have Had Oral Sex," *Washington Post*, September 16, 2005.
6. Quoted in Friedman, "Teen Sex."
7. Cited in Jennie Yabroff, "The Myths of Teen Sex," *Newsweek*, June 9, 2008.
8. Cited in Yabroff, "The Myths of Teen Sex."
9. Yabroff, "The Myths of Teen Sex."
10. Yabroff, "The Myths of Teen Sex."
11. Quoted in Tamar Lewin, "Are These Parties for Real?," *New York Times*, June 30, 2005.
12. Quoted in Friedman, "Teen Sex."
13. David Brooks, "Public Hedonism and Private Restraint," *New York Times*, April 17, 2005.

OPPOSING VIEWPOINTS® SERIES

CHAPTER 1

Is Teen Dating Violence a Serious Problem?

Chapter Preface

On September 30, 2011, Abraham Lopez entered the courtyard of South East High in Los Angeles and stabbed his exgirlfriend, Cindi Santana, who died later at a nearby hospital. In the wake of her death, the Los Angeles Unified School District (LAUSD) passed an antiviolence initiative targeting teen dating violence, a program that will cost an estimated $2 million. According to LAUSD board member Steve Zimmer, "policy is not consolation, and policy can't reverse the tragedy, but what we're trying to do today is make sure that anywhere in this district, when someone comes forward, or a family comes over, that school will have the resources to make sure this never happens again."[1] This hindsight approach frustrates activists who have long claimed that teen dating violence is a serious problem requiring government-supported programs to educate young people on how to differentiate between healthy and dangerous relationships. Indeed, following Cindi's death, Marjorie Gilberg, executive director of Break the Cycle, a grassroots organization devoted to addressing teen dating violence, laments, "Cindi Santana and her family did everything right to ensure her safety and the system failed them. We all failed them. Responding appropriately to dating abuse requires parents, schools, community leaders, law enforcement and elected officials to work together and we were not ready."[2] While not unsympathetic to the families of teen dating violence victims, others argue that families should be responsible for teaching young people about relationships, not American schools. Indeed the debate over whether teen dating violence is a problem worthy of government intervention is reflective of other teen dating violence debates.

Teen dating violence activists have in fact successfully lobbied Congress to set aside federal money for educational programs about dating violence. Organizations such as the Family

Violence Prevention Fund testified before the Senate Judiciary Committee, citing studies that show that up to one in three adolescent girls in the United States has been a victim of physical, emotional, or verbal abuse from a dating partner. According to Dr. Elizabeth Miller, "Most teens don't understand what a healthy relationship is, often mistaking the controlling behaviors that characterize abuse for signs of love."[3] Thus, activists argue, education programs are necessary. However, at of the end of 2011, only fourteen states had passed laws requiring teen dating abuse prevention education that would tap federal funds. According to Tara Shabazz of the California Partnership to End Domestic Violence, "There is tremendous public support behind teen dating violence education, but legislators can't seem to muster the political will."[4]

Opponents of funding for programs to educate young people about healthy relationships do not deny that the deaths of young women at the hands of their dating partners are tragic. They argue instead that devoting federal funds to support such programs is wasteful and beyond the scope of government. Michael McCormick of the American Coalition for Fathers and Children says that talking about dating violence "is not in line with public education."[5] He fears that in reality these programs would focus less on reducing dating violence than perpetuate myths about male socialization that demonize men and support an antifamily, feminist agenda. Combating these ideas is a serious obstacle for those who support such programs. Organizations such as the California Partnership to End Domestic Violence, and Break the Cycle, claim that dating violence programs are not like sex education and have nothing to do with marriage or gender. Nevertheless, bills that require parental notification and opt-out clauses have stalled legislation in many states. According to Break the Cycle's Gilberg, "Bullying prevention programs don't require parental notification. Gang prevention programs don't require parental notification. Why should dating violence be singled out as a controversial subject?"[6]

The debate over these programs nevertheless continues. The authors in the following chapter explore these and other issues in answer to the question: is teen dating violence a serious problem? As state and federal programs compete for funds in today's struggling economic climate, the debate over the need for teen dating violence programs will likely remain heated.

Notes

1. "LAUSD Tackles Teen Dating Violence in the Wake of Cindi Santana's Death," *Huffington Post*, October 12, 2011.
2. Marjorie Gilberg, "Too Little Too Late?" *Huffington Post*, October 19, 2011.
3. Quoted in Colleen Perry, "Teen Dating Violence Is on the Rise: What You Need to Know Now," *Huffington Post*, June 2, 2010.
4. Quoted in Gilberg, "Too Little Too Late?"
5. Quoted in Pamela M. Prah, "Domestic Violence," *CQ Researcher*, January 6, 2006.
6. Gilberg, "Too Little Too Late?"

> "Teen dating violence can tip off
> a cascade of other negative health
> consequences, and it underscores the
> importance of prevention efforts."

Teen Dating Violence Is a Serious Problem

Sadie F. Dingfelder

In the following viewpoint, the author claims that many people are unaware of the prevalence of teen dating violence. Studies show that one in three teens has experienced an emotionally abusive relationship and one in five has experienced physical abuse, she maintains. Despite these facts, many dismiss claims of teen dating violence as childishness or blame the victim, she argues. To combat the lack of awareness, advocates—including the parents of murdered children—support laws that protect victims and educate teens, she asserts. Sadie F. Dingfelder is a writer for Monitor on Psychology, *a publication of the American Psychological Association.*

As you read, consider the following questions:

1. What Texas law was passed due to the efforts of family members affected by teen dating violence, according to Dingfelder?

Sadie F. Dingfelder, "Ending an Epidemic," *Monitor on Psychology*, vol. 41, no. 3, March 2010, p. 32. Retrieved from: http://www.apa.org/monitor. Copyright © 2010 by the American Psychological Association. All rights reserved. Reproduced by permission.

2. What case does the author cite to support the claim that some people blame the victim for dating violence?

3. What did a 2006 report by the Centers for Disease Control and Prevention reveal about roughly 1.5 million teen victims of physical dating violence?

Few things thrill a 16-year-old more than being mistaken for a college student, and that was no exception for Jennifer Ann Crecente. Tagging along with her grandmother, Elizabeth Richeson, PhD, at APA's [American Psychological Association's] 2004 Annual Convention in Honolulu, Crecente glowed when famous psychologists asked her what university she attended and what her major was. "She told them all she wanted to be a psychologist," Richeson recalls.

No Clue to the Dangers

Crecente, an honors student and hospital volunteer, never had the chance to realize that dream. In February 2006, her ex-boyfriend, Justin Crabbe, shot her in the back of the head and left her bleeding in the woods near her home in Austin, Texas. Crecente's father, Drew, had no idea his daughter was in danger.

"I thought I was a pretty aware parent," he says. "I thought I knew about the major dangers she faced, and I had talked with her about drugs, about sex, about strangers when she was younger. But I just did not have any clue that one in three teens were being affected by abusive relationships."

After Jennifer's murder, Drew Crecente and Richeson clocked hundreds of hours researching teen dating violence, and they were shocked by its prevalence: Of teens who date, one in five report they have been hit, slapped or pushed by a partner, and almost a third say they've been involved in an emotionally abusive relationship, according to a 2006 survey of 1,004 teens, commissioned by Liz Claiborne Inc. A 2003 survey by the Centers for Disease Control and Prevention [CDC] of 14,956 high school students had a similar finding: According to results released in 2006, one in 11 high school students had been the victim of physical dating violence in the previous year.

An Unspoken Epidemic

Most people are surprised by these statistics, says Maritza Rivera, president of Aneesa Michelle's Group, a nonprofit organization that raises the public's awareness of teen dating violence. "It's an unspoken epidemic, and it's going on right in front of our faces," she says.

If Rivera, Crecente, Richeson and many others are successful, it won't be unspoken much longer. Through Aneesa Michelle's Group, which Rivera named after her niece—who was killed by her boyfriend in 2008—Rivera has given dozens of talks to high school students to challenge the belief that violence is an acceptable way to resolve conflicts. Crecente also started a nonprofit group, named for his daughter. Through Jennifer Ann's Group, Crecente and Richeson have helped pass a law in Texas: H.B. 121, which mandates that every school district in the state have a policy on intimate partner violence and provides a model policy that includes education and prevention.

Since that law passed in 2007, several other states have followed suit, including Rhode Island and, most recently, Ohio. Jennifer Ann's Group is also working to strengthen laws that protect teens with violent partners—by, for instance, allowing them to apply for protective orders on their own and ensuring harsh punishments for people who violate those orders.

Activists' efforts are working. Pediatricians have begun screening young patients for abusive relationships. The media increasingly covers dating violence. And this year [2010], Congress declared February to be "National Teen Dating Violence Awareness and Prevention Month"—a pronouncement that inspired hundreds of local agencies, state governments and nonprofit groups to redouble efforts to protect teens from intimate partner violence.

"We must teach our children what it means to have healthy relationships, free from harassment, fear and . . . abuse," says Sen. Mike Crapo (R-Idaho), who co-sponsored the Senate resolution that dedicated February to the cause.

The Rihanna Effect

Even though there have been many heartening successes, says Crecente, getting people to take teen dating violence seriously sometimes feels like an uphill battle. Most people are simply not aware of how common it is, and when they do become aware of it, they tend to dismiss it as teenage silliness or—even worse—blame the victim.

A case in point: Following the 2009 beating of pop star Rihanna by her boyfriend, fellow pop star Chris Brown, the Boston Public Health Commission polled 200 teens and found that almost half felt that the assault must have been Rihanna's fault. That poll came as no surprise to Rivera, who confronts those attitudes all too frequently when she gives presentations to high school students. "They'll say, 'Why did she keep arguing with him if she knew he was violent?'" Rivera says. "They say, 'She must have done something to make him so angry.'"

Of course, it's not just teens who can fail to take dating violence or its frequent precursor, abusive and manipulative behavior, seriously. When parents hear of harassing behavior, such as a teen being texted by her boyfriend dozens of times in an hour, asking where she is, who she's with and what's she doing, parents may dismiss it as puppy love, says Richeson. Teens may even interpret such jealous behavior as romantic. "Teens don't always have a strong sense of self, and they sometimes don't know what a healthy relationship is," she says. "Or, they would rather have an unpleasant relationship than not have one at all."

That intuition is backed up by research in the September 2009 *Violence Against Women*. In the study, CDC researchers convened 12 focus groups of middle-school students and asked them about romantic relationships. The researchers found that most

Who Perpetrates Teen Dating Violence?

The following data were drawn from two studies: the Toledo Adolescent Relationship Study and Suffolk County Study of Dating Aggression in High Schools.

 Mutual aggression

Girls are the sole perpetrators

Boys are the sole perpetrators

How girls in physically aggressive relationships see it

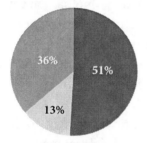

Toledo Adolescent Relationship Study

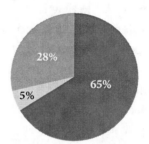

Suffolk County Study of Dating Aggression in High Schools

How boys in physically aggressive relationships see it

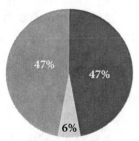

Toledo Adolescent Relationship Study

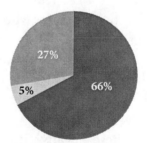

Suffolk County Study of Dating Aggression in High Schools

TAKEN FROM: Carrie Mulford and Peggy C. Giordanu, "Teen Dating Violence: A Closer Look at Adolescent Romantic Relationships," *NIJ Journal*, October 2008.

students did not condone relationship violence, but they did tend to endorse a view that girls are expected to meet boys' emotional and physical needs and not expect much in return—a power differential that can lead to coercive and violent behavior, says Rita Noonan, PhD, a CDC sociologist who authored the study.

Feeling Powerless

Power imbalance also puts teens at risk for health problems, says Emilio Ulloa, PhD, a psychology professor at San Diego State University. Ulloa, with his student Christina Buelna, surveyed 290 college students and found that victims of interpersonal violence were more likely to report feeling powerless in their relationships and to contract sexually transmitted infections, according to the study published in the *Journal of Interpersonal Violence*.

"Victims of interpersonal violence are less likely to have equal footing with their partners," says Ulloa. "They may be less likely to complain if their boyfriend has multiple partners, less likely to refuse to participate in sexual activity and more likely to be coerced into it."

The 2006 CDC report had a related finding: The roughly 1.5 million school students who've been the victim of physical dating violence in the previous year were more likely to have sex, binge drink, get into fights and attempt suicide. The study suggests that teen dating violence can tip off a cascade of other negative health consequences, and it underscores the importance of prevention efforts, Noonan says.

"All these negative health outcomes are preventable. They are not a natural part of teenage life," says Noonan. "Our young people deserve a bright and healthy future."

Raising Awareness of Teen Dating Violence

Though researchers are working on many different tactics for preventing teen dating violence, most scientists and activists agree that the problem must be confronted simultaneously at multiple levels—through schools, parents and peers. To that end, Jennifer Ann's Group is teaching teens, parents and other influential adults about the signs of teen partner violence, and how to respond to it. In particular, they have been distributing wallet cards that outline 10 signs of an abusive relationship and four steps for creating a safety plan. The card also lists a 24-hour, toll-free helpline.

"I wanted to make a card that is discreet. You can carry it in your wallet and it looks like a credit card," says Crecente. "It's also durable, so you can pass it along from friend to friend." Hundreds of school groups, church groups and activists have requested the cards, including Rivera of Aneesa Michelle's Group, who passed out the Spanish-language version at the Puerto Rican Day parade in New York last summer.

Such education efforts are vital to ensuring teens' safety, says Julia da Silva, director of APA's Office of Violence Prevention. "We know that most of the time physical and emotional violence against women is committed by someone they know, and it's important to help women recognize the warning signs," she says.

Keeping teens safe, while also making them less likely to put up with abuse as adults, is Richeson's ultimate goal. Between therapy sessions at her private practice in El Paso, Texas, she'll deliver cards to gynecologists' and pediatricians' offices. She's also given many talks about teen dating violence to high school students, school nurses and administrators—to just about anyone who will listen.

"I'm working on creating a speakers bureau of psychologists who can give these talks, raise awareness and maybe even save lives," she says.

Psychologists can also help by screening their clients—especially young ones—for abusive relationships at intake every year and whenever a client's relationship status has changed. That exact screening policy, she adds, was passed by the American Academy of Pediatrics last year, and Richeson hopes psychologists will follow suit.

"Teens aren't typically going to volunteer this kind of information," she says. "You have to ask them directly." Since the tragedy that turned them into crusaders against teen dating violence, Richeson and Crecente have sometimes felt overwhelmed by the extent of the problem. But it's the trickle of e-mails they receive, from a teen who found their informational card and realized that it was time to leave an abusive relationship, or a parent who was inspired to give his daughter the talk that Crecente wishes he'd known to give, that keeps them going.

"There's nothing we can do to bring Jennifer back," says Crecente. "But at least we can try to keep other families from going through what we did."

> *"The large majority of teens have never experience[d] the controlling behavior or physical, sexual, verbal, or emotional violence characteristic of dating abuse even once."*

The Problem of Teen Dating Violence Is Exaggerated

Mike Males

Teen dating violence is not a growing problem, argues the author of the following viewpoint. In fact, he claims, surveys show the opposite to be true. Nevertheless, organizations use exaggeration techniques to market their dating abuse programs, the author maintains. For example, he asserts, program advocates expand the definition of abuse to include such things as being told by their dating partner how to dress. Such exaggerations, he reasons, teach teens that normal disagreements amount to abuse and downplay the very serious violence that occurs at home. Mike Males, a senior researcher at the Center on Juvenile and Criminal Justice, is the author of The Scapegoat Generation: America's War on Adolescents.

As you read, consider the following questions:

1. According to Males, what do long-term measures such as the National Crime Victimization Survey reveal about teen crime?
2. How, in the author's view, did the Claiborne survey expand the definition of "relationship"?
3. What are some of the exaggeration techniques used by dating abuse program advocates, according to the author?

American secondary schools are coming under intense pressure from corporations, politicians, and the news media to implement prescribed "teenage dating abuse" programs. A recent resolution by the National Association of Attorneys General [NAAG] urged "school districts to incorporate dating violence education into health education curriculums in middle and/or high school." "We are committed to addressing this issue through education," declared Rhode Island Attorney General Patrick Lynch, the resolution's chief sponsor. "A curriculum such as Liz Claiborne, Inc.'s Love Is Not Abuse is an effective way to begin the process of education, prevent abuse and help to save lives."

Looking at Commonly Cited Numbers

But is teen dating abuse "increasing" to "staggering" levels, as program advocates insist, justifying entire new school curriculums to combat it? Commonly cited numbers reported in the press and by program advocates, summarized by the American Bar Association's Teen Dating Violence Initiative, indeed appear alarming. "A comparison of Intimate Partner Violence rates between teens and adults reveals that teens are at higher risk of intimate partner abuse. . . . Approximately 1 in 5 female high school students report being physically and/or sexually abused by a dating partner. . . ." "Females ages 16–24 are more vulnerable to intimate partner violence than any other age group—at a rate almost triple the national average."

However, the most alarming numbers being cited reflect 1990s data. More recent numbers from larger surveys are considerably lower. In 2003, the Youth Risk Behavior Survey found 9% of students in grades 9–12 reported having a dating partner "hit, slap, or physically hurt you on purpose" at least once. In 2005, the Bureau of Justice Statistics' Intimate Partner Violence report found that 2.1% of students ages 12–19 (including 0.9% of youths age 12–15, and 3.4% of those age 16–19) experienced any form of physical violence (murder, simple assault, aggravated assault, rape, robbery, or sexual assault) from an intimate partner (a spouse, ex-spouse, boyfriend/girlfriend, ex-boyfriend/girlfriend, same-sex partner). This report relied on the National Crime Victimization Survey [NCVS], America's largest, most consistent, and only long-term measure of such crime, with samples of more than 70,000 Americans every year since 1993.

A 2008 survey commissioned by Liz Claiborne, Inc., a fashion corporation that markets dating abuse [education] programs, found similar levels for younger students. Its survey of 1,043 students age 11–14 found that 2% of 11–14-year-olds (14 males and 7 females) reported ever having had a partner "hit, slap, punch, choke, or kick" them and 1% reported having been pressured into sexual activity (five males and eight females; whether these duplicated some of those physically abused is not shown).

Teens Are Not at Greater Risk

Recent surveys do not find teens uniquely at risk. The Intimate Partner Violence survey finds that in the most recent five years, 2001–05, teens age 16–19 had lower rates of intimate-partner violence (3.4%) than adults age 20–24 (6.5%) and 25–34 (4.7%) and somewhat above adults age 35–49 (2.8%), while 12–15-year-olds experienced the lowest levels of dating violence (0.9%) of any age except 65 and older (less than 0.1%). Given that intimate partner violence rises sharply as socioeconomic status falls and that teenagers and young adults suffer considerably higher rates of poverty and socioeconomic disadvantage than older adults, teens appear to experience fairly low rates of intimate partner violence for their demographics.

Nor is dating abuse rising. The long-term measures available, such as FBI [Federal Bureau of Investigation] Uniform Crime Reports, Monitoring the Future, and the National Crime Victimization Survey, variously agree that murder, rape, robbery, assault, sexual assault, and kidnapping involving both younger and older teens have dropped dramatically over the last 10 to 20 years, most to all-time lows. Intimate partner violence has fallen the most dramatically. The NCVS found that from 1993 to 2005, the proportion of teenage females reporting intimate partner violence fell by 70%.

These seemingly calming trends and numbers have not moderated program advocates' alarms, however. "One in three teens reports knowing a friend or peer who has been hit, punched, kicked, slapped or physically hurt by their dating partner," a representative of Liz Claiborne stated. "The number of tweens [ages 11 to 12] in abusive relationships (is) staggering." NAAG's 2008 resolution agreed: "Teen dating violence has become a prevalent problem in high schools, junior high schools and middle schools throughout our country. . . . Recent studies have shown that teen dating violence is starting" as young as ages "11 to 14."

Using Questionable Techniques

Investigation reveals that program advocates have used several questionable techniques with troubling implications for responsible programming to drastically exaggerate the prevalence of teen dating abuse. In particular, advocates have extended the definition of "teen dating violence" far beyond NAAG's criterion of "a pattern of controlling and abusive behavior of one person over another within a romantic relationship including verbal, emotional, physical, sexual and financial abuse."

Program advocates' first exaggeration technique, aside from including figures for 20–24-year-olds (an age group with considerably higher violence rates) as "teenage dating violence" and continuing to repeat higher 1990s numbers, is to cite one-time behaviors rather than those documenting a "pattern of controlling and abusive behavior." As will be seen, a girl saying something to make the boy sitting next to her in class feel bad about himself could constitute "dating abuse" by Liz Claiborne's definition.

The second exaggeration technique is to emphasize not the small numbers of teens who report actually being abused, but secondhand guesses by teens in response to speculative questions as to whether "people your age" might suffer abuse by dating partners. Thus, while 2% of 11–14-year-olds reported being abused, 20% speculated that undefined peers might experience dating abuse. Of course, guesses about what others "your age" are experiencing can be inflated by one case known to many students, gossip, rumors, and media reports.

Program advocates' third and most disturbing exaggeration technique is to expand the definitions of "relationship" and "abuse" substantially beyond behaviors normally associated with the terms. In Claiborne's survey, a "relationship" includes not just regular dating, but "sitting next to each other in school," "admitting that he/she likes the other person," "flirting," and "calling or texting each other regularly." "Abuse" includes partners who "made you feel bad or embarrassed about yourself," "made you feel nervous about doing something he/she doesn't like," "hurt you with words," or "tried to tell you how to dress"—even once.

Alarming Data from Small Samples

Finally, the most alarming dating abuse numbers come from tiny subsamples of teens, not the whole sample. For example, consider Claiborne's statement, "69% of all teens who had sex by age 14 said they have gone through one or more types of abuse in a relationship." Having "sex" referred to not just intercourse or oral sex, but ever "having gone further than kissing and making out." "Abuse," as noted, was defined to include just about any problem. Thus, the "69%" figure actually referred to around 30 of the 1,043 youths surveyed who had experienced even the mildest negative interaction with a partner with whom they had gone further than kissing or making out.

Claiborne's survey found the percentages of teens suffering verbal and emotional abuse, violent threats, and extreme jealousy from a dating or "hookup" partner rare as well. Just 8% had a partner who ever (even once) "asked you to only spend time with him/her," "called you names or put you down" (7%), "hurt you with words" (6%), or "threatened to spread rumors about you" (4%). For behaviors more commonly considered emotionally abusive and controlling, just 3% of teens had "been concerned about your safety (being hurt physically because of him/her)" and 2% reported that a dating or hookup partner actually had "threatened to hurt you or himself/herself if you were to break up."

Nor does the survey confirm Claiborne's and news media assertions that modern communications technology has opened up vast new theaters of meanness. Only 2% of 11–12-year-olds and 7% of 13–14-year-olds had ever had a partner say anything "really mean" about them using cellphones, text messages, instant messaging, social sites, blogs, or other Internet tools one or more times.

If program advocates' own recent survey is credible, then, the large majority of teens have never experience[d] the controlling behavior or physical, sexual, verbal, or emotional violence characteristic of dating abuse even once, let alone as a pattern of mistreatment. Abuses appear to be rare and dropping, not epidemic and rising. Around one in 50 younger teens and one in 30 older teens report intimate partner violence in a year's time, levels similar to those among adults.

Wasting Resources to Present Harmful Biases

Should schools adopt prescribed dating abuse programs, then? Aside from the budget and time-on-task issues entailed in adding full-scale dating abuse programs to already overloaded high school curriculums amid funding cutbacks, the deceptions advocates have used to market these programs present troubling indicators of potentially harmful biases underlying these curriculums.

First, the extreme exaggerations marketers employ lend the impression that violence is normative to teen relationships. They stereotype even very young students as promiscuous, violent, and cruel. Such negative stereotypes toward young people do not connote the attitude of respect programs should seek to inculcate.

Second, program advocates' overbroad definitions risk teaching students the unrealistic lesson that normal, occasional disagreements and unharmonious feelings constitute "abuse" and that healthy relationships must always be blissful. Even the soundest adult marriages would be rated as abusive according to Claiborne's definitions.

Finally, by ignoring or downplaying uncomfortable precursors such as parental, household, and community violence in favor of more comfortable, superficial explanations, programs obscure important causes. For example, Claiborne representatives blame tweens' "early sexual experimentation" as the cause of "increased levels of teen dating violence and abuse." However, aside from strong evidence that both teenage and adult "intimate partner violence has been declining," a solid body of research indicates that growing up in violent homes and suffering childhood violence and sexual abuse, usually inflicted by parents or caretakers, is the most reliable predictor of early sexual activity, violence, and abuse. The latest Child Maltreatment report substantiated 200,000 violent and sexual abuses and 100,000 emotional abuses inflicted on children and youths by parents in 2006.

Dating violence is not increasing or "epidemic" among high school students but does affect a fraction. It does not appear to be a distinct form of violence, but part of a continuum that includes abusive parents and violent homes and communities. This indicates that for most schools, targeted referral and counseling training, services, and curriculums that include dating violence as one type of health risk, rather than full-scale programs dedicated solely to dating violence, represent the most viable educational approach. Whatever strategies are adopted in violence prevention education, the most accurate information rather than unwarranted exaggerations and a respectful approach toward young people rather than negative stereotypes are required.

> "*Young women today are unequipped with the knowledge they need to sense when something in a relationship is off.*"

Many Teens Lack the Knowledge Needed to Recognize Potential Abusers

Rachel Aydt

Although teen dating abuse may be a serious problem, asserts the author of the following viewpoint, identifying risky dating partners is difficult for naïve teens. In fact, many dating abusers are very charming, and that is one way they manipulate their partners, she reports. Once involved in the relationship, an abuser becomes jealous of the victim's other relationships and tries to dictate the victim's life, the author maintains. Unfortunately, she argues, many dismiss the seriousness of dating violence or claim that the victim provoked the abuse. Because identifying abusers is so challenging for teens, education programs are necessary, she concludes. Rachel Aydt is a writer who lives in New York City.

As you read, consider the following questions:

1. What evidence does Aydt provide to show that that Megan's story of dating violence is not unique?

2. What did Megan conclude when she found out her ex-boyfriend David was seen hitting his new girl-friend?

3. What does the author report shocked middle school teacher Katie Seltzer when she heard how her students were talking about the Rihanna incident?

"The first time David looked at me was the first time I felt beautiful," remembers Megan,* 18, from Austin, Texas. "He was such a gentleman. He would carry my books, and say, 'Hey, Gorgeous,' when he called."

Megan may have been in heaven with her new BF [boyfriend], but it would only be weeks before things took a dangerous turn. Soon, David's cooing tone changed, and phone calls became abusive, starting in the morning with, "Hey, b----, why are you still in bed? What the hell's wrong with you?"

Sadly, Megan's story is not unique. According to the *Chicago Tribune*, one in 10 teen girls suffer dating violence in their relationships. And in another poll conducted by the organization Love Is Respect, one in five teens who have been in a serious relationship reported being hit, slapped or pushed by their partner. And after [pop singer] Rihanna showed up swollen and beaten in the tabloids, allegedly at the hands of boyfriend Chris Brown [also a pop singer], dating violence has been a hot topic in conversations around the country.

Why does abuse seem to be popping up everywhere? Erin Weed, founder of the self-defense organization Girls Fight Back, has this theory: "I travel all over teaching self-defense to girls, and what I'm seeing everywhere I go is a lack of boundaries. Young women today are unequipped with the knowledge they need to sense when something in a relationship is off," she says. "And so they just don't notice when a manipulative person enters their world."

* Name has been changed.

Defining Abuse

But detecting a potentially dangerous person isn't always an easy task. After all, the most troubled guys can seem totally cool on the outside—Chris Brown is a perfect example.

"Abusers aren't always the bad boys," says Ann Burke, a middle school health teacher and dating violence activist whose daughter, Lindsay, was murdered by her abuser. "They can be anywhere. They are the community leaders, the popular guys, even the captains of the football team. You just can't tell who is capable of violence. On the surface they might be totally charming, but their charm ends up being a huge part of how they manipulate you."

And how are these people able to go about manipulating you exactly? "Well, 30 texts a day from a guy isn't normal," says Weed. She goes on to explain that some relationship abuse is verbal, which means that victims will be called names, talked down to, belittled or cursed at. Other relationship abuse escalates to full-blown physical violence. Whether it's verbal, physical or both, it is dangerous and should never be tolerated.

When Abuse Escalates

Megan's relationship was tainted by classic verbal abuse and bullying. "Every day I would go to David's house after school, without thinking twice about whether I could go home or see a friend instead," she says. "When we weren't at his house, we were at his football practice where I was a water girl. If I didn't fill the water fast enough, he'd start to yell at me."

David began to watch Megan's every move and would express jealousy over something as simple as her getting a text from a friend.

"Sometimes when he'd call me, he'd scream and then put me on hold for an hour," Megan recalls. "He would say hurtful things about being with other girls, and when I'd start to cry, he'd apologize and tell me that he'd change. I began to feel scared of him. He was a foot taller than me."

Megan knew she wanted to leave the relationship, but it took four attempts before she could end it for good. "Every time we broke up, he'd tell me he needed me. He even said that if I left him he would kill himself," she says.

They ultimately broke up, and several months later David was seen hitting his new girlfriend (with whom he'd cheated on Megan) in the school cafeteria. "I heard that and knew that if we'd stayed together that could have been me," says Megan. Now, she's hoping to help out other victims like herself by working for an abuse hotline.

Innocent Beginnings Can Lead to Danger

Nicci,* 18, also from Austin, first developed feelings for Michael,* whom she describes as the class clown, when she was in summer school.

"I was shy, and he started talking to me," Nicci recalls. "It didn't take long before we were a couple. One day, we were over at his house, and his mom let it slip that he'd been in anger management courses. She made him tell me why."

What quickly came to light was his history of two assault charges, which he'd racked up for hurting former girlfriends. "That was fine with me, because I knew he was getting help. What I didn't know was that he'd dropped out of his group," says Nicci.

Soon, Michael fell into his old habits. Recalls Nicci, "He was always extremely jealous. He'd answer my cell when my best friend called and say, 'She can't talk because she's with me.' He wouldn't let me spend the night at her house, because he'd irrationally think something was going to happen between me and her, or between me and one of my guy friends."

Michael's abuse quickly escalated from verbal to physical. "He would always demand physical attention, and if I didn't feel like making out with him, he'd say, 'If you don't give it to me, I can just go get it somewhere else.'"

Who Is at Risk?

Studies show that people who harm their dating partners are more depressed and are more aggressive than peers. Other factors that increase risk for harming a dating partner include:

- Trauma symptoms
- Alcohol use
- Having a friend involved in dating violence
- Having problem behaviors in other areas
- Belief that dating violence is acceptable
- Exposure to harsh parenting
- Exposure to inconsistent discipline
- Lack of parental supervision, monitoring, and warmth

Centers for Disease Control and Prevention, "Understanding Teen Dating Violence Fact Sheet," 2010.

Michael would also tell her how to dress, preferably in clothing that wasn't too revealing. "Makeup had to be minimal, and sleeves had to be long," Nicci remembers.

From Bad to Worse

Nicci and Michael eventually broke up, but, as with many abusive relationships, the problems didn't end there.

"We still had all the same friends, and one night I showed up at his house to hang out and watch a movie with everyone. Before I came over I'd even gone shopping for his favorite foods. He told me to leave, but I refused. I didn't think it was fair," Nicci says. "He called me a terrible name, threw a pair of scissors at me, grabbed me by the hair and threw me against the stairs."

I Like Boys Cartoon. © Copyright 2010, by Daryl Cagle and Cagle Cartoons.

Despite the fact that other people were there, no one did anything to stop him. "I was screaming for help because he hit me in the jaw," Nicci says. "I managed to escape to my car, but I was blocked in by a van. Michael chased me, jumped into my car and proceeded to scream at me and hit me in the face. He damaged my tear ducts, and to this day I still can't tear up the way I used to."

Dying for Love

While Nicci's injuries were scary, she otherwise escaped from the relationship without any serious lasting physical harm. Some girls aren't so lucky. Take Lindsay Burke, for example. A beautiful and compassionate young woman, Lindsay became involved with Gerardo Martinez after meeting him at a wedding in 2003. Her mom remembers her being flattered by his compliments and his undivided attention, and Lindsay became instantly smitten. Their relationship grew intense very quickly. Before long, Lindsay was living a secret nightmare.

During their two-year relationship, Lindsay's mom, Ann, did notice an extreme personality change in her daughter, but she wasn't sure what she could do about it.

"I noticed things that didn't seem right. Lindsay and Gerardo became very involved, very quickly. She would have these long phone calls every single day with him, which didn't seem normal for a healthy relationship. She had always been an upbeat and social girl, but she became withdrawn and sad."

Concerned, Mrs. Burke discussed the situation with three counselors, but the first two said nothing about abuse. The third one pulled out a list of abusive relationship warning signs . . . but it was too late. In 2005, after a rocky relationship riddled with every warning sign of abuse, Gerardo murdered Lindsay. He was convicted and is serving out his sentences—spending the rest of his life in prison without parole.

Education Against Abuse

Sadly, there are so many stories like that of Megan, Nicci and Lindsay, but many people—both girls and guys—often underestimate and even dismiss how serious dating violence is. Katie Seltzer, a middle school teacher at an all-girls school in New York City, was shocked in February [2009] to hear the way her students were talking about the Rihanna incident.

"Some of the girls were saying that they didn't think Chris Brown had done anything, and that Rihanna had bitten herself for attention," says Seltzer. "Most said that even if he did beat her, she probably 'deserved it,' and his behavior toward her wouldn't affect their choice about whether to buy his music or not."

It's this ignorance that has prompted Seltzer to take the time to open up a dialogue about the common traits of dating violence in all of her health classes. "It's important for girls to understand that healthy relationships are based on respect, not on manipulation," she says.

Lindsay's mom felt so strongly about the need to educate people that she worked to pass the Lindsay Ann Burke Act. It requires every school in Rhode Island to educate all students in grades seven to 12 about dating violence. It's the first law of its kind in the country, and there are currently [2009] eight other states with similar laws pending.

"We must understand that abuse can happen to anyone, just like it did to our Lindsay," explains Mrs. Burke. "We must educate ourselves so we can begin to stop the violence."

> *"It's not unusual for kids—both boys and girls—to say it's OK to hit your girlfriend or boyfriend."*

Some Teens Believe Teen Dating Violence Is Normal

Megan Twohey and Bonnie Miller Rubin

Some teens believe that abuse is a normal part of dating, claim the authors of the following viewpoint. In fact, they maintain, these attitudes are part of a broader acceptance of intimate partner violence. Overcoming these attitudes is a challenge, as dating violence is underreported, they assert. To overcome cultural stereotypes about dating violence, encourage healthy relationships, and help the one in ten teens who suffer dating abuse, the authors argue that states should fund teen dating violence education programs. Megan Twohey and Bonnie Miller Rubin are reporters for the Chicago Tribune.

As you read, consider the following questions:

1. According to Ed Loos, what was a common reaction among students at Lake Forest High School to Chris Brown's alleged attack on Rihanna?

2. Why did the incident between Chris Brown and Rihanna create so much interest among teens, in the authors' opinion?

3. Why do the authors believe that teen victims require unique interventions?

Ed Loos, a junior at Lake Forest High School, said a common reaction among students to [pop singer] Chris Brown's alleged attack on [pop singer and girlfriend] Rihanna goes something like this: "Ha! She probably did something to provoke it."

In Chicago, Sullivan High School sophomore Adeola Matanmi has heard the same.

"People said, 'I would have punched her around too,'" Matanmi said. "And these were girls!"

A Need for Education

As allegations of battery swirl around the famous couple, experts on domestic violence say the response from teenagers just a few years younger shows the desperate need to educate this age group about dating violence.

Their acceptance, or even approval, of abuse in romantic relationships is not a universal reaction. But it comes at a time when 1 in 10 teenagers has suffered such abuse and females ages 16 to 24 experience the highest rates of any age group, research shows.

In recent years, some schools and youth organizations have started educating teens about the dangers of dating violence. Rhode Island and Virginia have adopted laws requiring such instruction in the public schools.

But most states, including Illinois, don't have such a mandate, and education on the topic remains in short supply, experts say. Two of three new programs created by the federal Violence Against Women Act in 2005 to address teen dating violence were never funded.

Teen Power and Control Wheel

The Power and Control Wheel illustrates behavioral patterns that are used by abusive partners to establish and maintain control over the other person and that can lead to physical and sexual violence, such as:

Anger/ Emotional Abuse	Putting him/her down • Making him/her feel badly about him or herself • Name calling • Making him/ her think he/she's crazy • Playing mind games • Humiliating him/her • Making him/her feel guilty
Using Social Status	Treater her like a servant • Making all the decisions • Acting like the "master of the castle" • Being the one to define men's and women's roles
Intimidation	Making someone afraid by using looks, actions, gestures • Smashing things • Destroying property • Abusing pets • Displaying weapons
Minimize/ Deny/Blame	Making light of the abuse and not taking concerns about it seriously • Saying the abuse didn't happen • Shifting responsibility for abusive behavior • Saying he/she caused it
Threats	Making and/or carrying out threats to do something to hurt another • Threatening to leave, to commit suicide, to report him/her to the police • Making him/her drop charges • Making him/her do illegal things
Sexual Coercion	Manipulating or making threats to get sex • Getting her pregnant • Threatening to take the children away • Getting someone drunk or drugged to have sex
Isolation/ Exclusion	Controlling what another does, who he/she sees, and talks to, what he/she reads, where he/she goes • Limiting outside involvement • Using jealousy to justify actions
Peer Pressure	Threatening to expose someone's weakness or spread rumors • Telling malicious lies about an individual to peer group

TAKEN FROM: Michigan Domestic Violence Prevention and Treatment Board, "Teen Power and Control Wheel," Adapted from the Domestic Abuse Intervention in Duluth, Minnesota, n.d.

"This incident has brought the issue into sharp focus," said Esta Soler, president of the California-based Family Violence Prevention Fund. "This type of education is not happening in any broad or consistent way. We need to take it to scale, to make sure it's happening in every community."

Details of the incident between singers Brown and Rihanna are fuzzy, but the story continues to create much buzz among teens across the Chicago area. Because she's 21 and he's 19, many teens see them as peers.

Katie Lullo, a junior at Elk Grove High School, said her classmates and friends were upset. "No one thinks it's right for a guy to hit a girl," she said. And when the topic arose at an after-school program at Evanston's YMCA, many participants said abuse was "bogus."

But other teens insist violence is sometimes justified in relationships.

Cultural Acceptance of Abuse

While young fans have plastered Rihanna's MySpace page with notes of support, many comments on Brown's page express delight at the possibility that he battered a woman.

Kriana Jackson, a sophomore at Sullivan, said it's a sign of a broader culture of acceptance of abuse.

"There was a girl at school this week with a scratch on her eye," Jackson said. "She was talking openly about her boyfriend hitting her, but she was smiling and saying it was funny."

Young people carry these attitudes into adulthood, experts say, and young targets of dating violence are more likely to succumb to aggression in later relationships.

For that reason, experts see education and other prevention initiatives geared at teens and preteens as one of the best hopes for halting dating and domestic violence.

"We know that education is absolutely crucial to breaking the cycle of abuse and strengthening healthy relationships," said Candice Hopkins, director of loveisrespect.org, the National

Teen Dating Abuse Helpline, which started in 2007 and receives about 90 contacts a week.

Moving in a Different World

Because young victims move in a different world than that of older people, they require unique interventions.

Text messaging and online social-networking sites, especially popular among teenagers, serve as tools for stalking and harassment. Victims often keep quiet, fearing that if they report another student's aggressive behavior, they will be socially ostracized—or that their parents will confiscate their cell phone or close a Facebook account.

Teens also can have a harder time severing contact with an abuser. Many are forced to see the perpetrator every day at school, sometimes in the same class. Young adults seeking an order of protection from Cook County judges must bring a guardian to apply on their behalf.

Last summer [2008], the president of the National Association of Attorneys General launched a campaign called "Working Together to End the Violence" and specifically called on communities to focus on relationship abuse among young people. More recently, the Family Violence Prevention Fund launched a national public-service advertising campaign this month [February 2009] called "That's Not Cool" to help teens recognize digital dating abuse and take steps to prevent it.

The Chicago-based group Between Friends is among the non-profit organizations that go into schools to teach students about the signs of abusive control, why it's wrong and how to cultivate heathy relationships.

"When we first get there, it's not unusual for kids—both boys and girls—to say it's OK to hit your girlfriend or boyfriend," said Kathy Doherty, the organization's executive director. "By the time we're done, they say, yes, it is abuse, and, no, we shouldn't do that."

As Doherty and others work to expand such programming, they hope teachers, parents and others use the story about Brown and Rihanna to talk to teens about dating violence.

Loos said his law teacher at Lake Forest recently incorporated the story into class.

But when students brought it up in Chelsea Whitis' economics class at Lane Tech High School in Chicago, the teacher brushed it aside.

"He said the celebrities were getting too much attention and didn't want us to talk about it," Whitis said.

| "All students, no matter where they reside or their background, deserve to be educated about [dating violence] in order to protect themselves and others."

Teen Dating Violence Education Programs Should Be Mandatory

Ann Burke

The author of the following viewpoint maintains that no matter a person's educational, socioeconomic, or ethnic background, anyone can be a victim or an abuser in intimate relationships. Thus, she argues, all students should learn about dating violence so that they can protect themselves. Comprehensive programs that help students identify the warning signs of abuse and promote healthy relationships are in fact working, she claims. Thus, Violence Against Women Act funds should be devoted to prevention of teen dating violence. Ann Burke, whose daughter, Lindsay, was murdered by Lindsay's ex-boyfriend, is president and founder of the Lindsay Ann Burke Memorial Fund and the co-founder of the Love Is Not Abuse Coalition.

Ann Burke, "Testimony of Ann Burke, R.N., M.Ed., President and Founder, Lindsay Ann Burke Memorial Fund, and Co-Founder of the Love Is Not Abuse Coalition," Field Hearing of US Senate Judiciary Committee, June 3, 2011.

As you read, consider the following questions:

1. Which state was the first to pass a comprehensive teen dating violence law, according to Burke?
2. What does the author say is necessary to truly prevent another tragedy like the death of her daughter, Lindsay?
3. What does a report released by the World Health Organization say is the one effective strategy to prevent actual violence?

I speak to you today as a mother, an advocate, and retired teacher. It has been almost six years since my daughter, Lindsay, a 23-year-old aspiring teacher, was brutally tortured and murdered by her ex-boyfriend. We cannot change the past, but we can help shape and determine the future. And so, I am proud that we have created a positive legacy in honor of Lindsay. In 2007, Rhode Island became the first state to pass a comprehensive teen dating violence law; now, at least 14 states have followed the example of the Lindsay Ann Burke Act and passed laws to support education on teen dating violence. Many times, the states passed laws after other parents experienced my same nightmare.

A Parent's Nightmare

I know many of these parents from across our nation. We have a parent email support group; a group no one wants to belong to. And today, I speak for them as well as myself. Not only do we live with the tremendous loss of our daughters and sons, but we have all been traumatized by the horrendous, horrific manner in which many of our children were tortured and murdered. Suffice it to say that the details of dating violence murders are beyond any sense of decency and morality.

Just like the victims of dating violence, we come from all walks of life, crossing lines of race, socioeconomics, and education. Anyone can be a victim and anyone can be an abuser. And that's precisely why I feel so strongly, both as a parent and a teacher, that *all* students, no matter where they reside or their background, deserve to be educated about this topic in order to protect themselves and others.

In Rhode Island, the attention given to this subject has made a difference. Since the passage of the Lindsay Ann Burke Act, physical teen dating violence rates have decreased from 14 percent in 2007 to 10 percent in 2009 (CDC [Centers for Disease Control and Prevention] Youth Risk Behavior Survey). Just as importantly, the law created awareness on the severity of the issue among school personnel. Now, teachers are more receptive to teaching the topic of healthy relationships in health class. Before the law, it was unclear where and whether this subject should be addressed.

Success Stories Arise out of Tragedy

The Lindsay Ann Burke Memorial Fund has worked to address dating violence primarily through educating teachers, parents, and students. The stigma of hiding abuse is being lifted. The lack of awareness of abusive behaviors is ending. Beyond the statistics, I'd like to share some real-life success stories. When speaking with student groups, invariably one or two students will disclose that they are in or have been in an abusive relationship. Since teaching the topic of dating violence in my own classroom, I have heard from several former students who told me how their education helped them and their friends to identify their relationships as abusive and get out of those relationships safely. One student wrote me a two-page letter about the abusive relationship she found herself in. The last paragraph reads, "So I wrote this letter because I'll always wonder how long my initial relationship with that boy would have lasted if I hadn't had your voice in my head warning me to get out quickly. I think that if you had never taught me all of the warning signs of an abusive relationship, I would have strived to be a better girlfriend and I would have let him control me because I wouldn't have known better. I'd never had a real boyfriend before, so how would I know the difference?

Teens' Perspectives May Influence Dating Violence

Young men may believe:

- they have the right to "control" their female partners in any way necessary
- "masculinity" is physical aggressiveness
- they "possess" their partner . . .

Young women may believe:

- they are responsible for solving problems in their relationships
- their boyfriend's jealousy, possessiveness and even physical abuse, is "romantic"
- abuse is "normal" . . .
- there is no one to ask for help

Alabama Coalition Against Domestic Violence, "Dating Violence," n.d., www.acadv.org.

Anything could have happened last year. Thank you for teaching me those lessons. Keep doing what you're doing. You are truly making a difference."

Another health teacher received a letter from a former student who wrote, "Last year in health class we learned about healthy relationships . . . I listened . . . I'm glad I did because over the summer I realized that my boyfriend was starting to become abusive. He would call me 30 times a day, leaving me voicemails of him screaming at the top of his lungs. One day I couldn't hang out and he punched a wall, and threatened to do the same to me.

If I hadn't taken your health class, I would definitely still be with him. So thank you for teaching us about relationships. It really does matter. People don't think it happens in our school, it does." Another health teacher told me that after he finished teaching his unit on dating violence one student walked up to him after class, pulled up the sleeve of her shirt exposing several bruises and said, "This is what my boyfriend did to me."

A Comprehensive Approach

As we have learned, it is not enough to ask teachers to add on a brief, one-time lesson or hold one assembly on dating violence. To truly prevent another tragedy like Lindsay, we need to start early and meet youth at every point of their day on an ongoing, consistent basis—in school, after school, in the community, and in the home.

There is no silver bullet, single message, intervention, or campaign that has been demonstrated to prevent teen dating violence. Success will require a comprehensive approach. But on a positive note, we know that prevention works. We have solid evidence that school-based teen dating violence prevention programs have been effective in changing behaviors.

Prevention research tells us we need to support education programs starting in middle school that do not simply talk about the warning signs of dating abuse but help initiate conversations about healthy relationships. We need to educate and engage those who influence teens, including parents, teachers, coaches, older youth, and others. Many times these leaders do not know the critical role they play in young people's lives and the power they have to promote healthy relationships and steer teens away from unhealthy ones. We need to meet youth where they are—in person but just as importantly online through social marketing campaigns and tools. And policies need to be adopted to support this programming.

The Lindsay Ann Burke Act required schools to adopt a teen dating violence policy. The implementation varies, but some schools in Rhode Island have adopted a strong prevention and intervention school policy. I worked with Futures Without Violence, formerly Family Violence Prevention Fund, and others to draft a national model middle school policy. This policy, based largely on the model policy developed by the Rhode Island Department of Education, is being advanced in communities across the country. There are a few core elements including school-wide prevention education, training programs for school personnel, parent engagement, innovative intervention strategies to respond to abuse, and partnerships with community agencies to help victims of abuse.

Investing in Prevention

Why is teen dating violence prevention an issue for the Violence Against Women Act [VAWA] and this committee? Last year [2010], we spent more than $400 million through the Department of Justice VAWA programs to combat the serious crimes of domestic violence, dating violence, sexual assault, and stalking. We need to invest in preventing teen dating violence to stop these crimes.

A recent report released by the World Health Organization said: "There is currently only one strategy for the prevention of domestic violence that can be classified *effective* at preventing actual violence. This is the use of school-based programs to prevent violence within *dating relationships*."

As a mother, I can still remember the deep pain in my heart five years ago, when I first learned that dating violence is a preventable health problem. My hope is that the reauthorization of the Violence Against Women Act continues to support and expand services for teen victims but also includes a focus on the prevention and early intervention of teen dating violence. By involving the whole community, we will recognize that teen dating violence is a real and serious issue that can be prevented.

> *"Students are spending precious class time role-playing dating scenarios rather than studying the grammar of dependent clauses or poring over algebra work sheets."*

School Teen Dating Violence Programs Are Unnecessary and Wasteful

Heather Mac Donald

Spending class time to discuss teen dating violence is wasteful and unproductive, claims the author of the following viewpoint. Although the death of a child is tragic, policy makers should question the deeper causes of teen dating violence, such as the breakdown of the family and the failure of school social service programs, she asserts. Teaching teens about dating is the responsibility of the family, the author maintains, and shifting that responsibility to schools will further marginalize parents and take time away from academic subjects that will actually help students escape destructive social patterns. Heather Mac Donald is a contributing editor to City Journal, *a publication of the free-market think tank the Manhattan Institute.*

As you read, consider the following questions:

1. According to Mac Donald, what percentage of Hispanic seventh-graders at Berendo Middle School were deemed proficient in California's English Language Arts test in 2010–11?

2. What is the attitude of the social services lobby toward promiscuity and family structure, in the author's view?

3. In the author's opinion, how does the *Los Angeles Times* prove that the media do not judge premature sexual activity?

If you wonder why American students rank poorly among industrialized nations on academic skills, here's part of the explanation, from a seventh-grade classroom in the Los Angeles Unified School District:

> On a recent morning, [reports the *Los Angeles Times*,] Trina Greene, manager of Peace Over Violence's Start Strong program, faced a class at Berendo Middle School in Pico-Union and dived into matters of love and control.
>
> She took students through an exercise in which they had to decide whether to leave a relationship. Under one scenario, a girl pinched a boy for looking at another girl. The students said they would end the relationship. But when she bought him a gold chain for his birthday, a number of them wavered, saying they might stay.

Only 35 percent of Hispanic seventh-graders at this overwhelmingly Hispanic middle school were deemed proficient in California's English Language Arts test in 2010–11, and only 43 percent were deemed proficient in Math. Yet Berendo's students are spending precious class time role-playing dating scenarios rather than studying the grammar of dependent clauses or poring over algebra work sheets. (The purchase of a gold chain in this dating scenario is interesting, since we can safely assume that the Start Strong program has been rigorously vetted for "cultural appropriateness." Taxpayers subsidize lunch for 96 percent of Berendo's students.)

Now comes a member of the Los Angeles Board of Education who wants every school in the Los Angeles public school system to teach students "how to recognize when a relationship is becoming abusive," according to the *Los Angeles Times*. Over the last several months [during the fall of 2011], L.A. Board of Education member Steve Zimmer, a former teacher and activist, has been working closely with the anti-dating-violence program Peace Over Violence on how to expand its services district-wide. The proposed expansion, estimated to cost $2 million in its first year and approximately $600,000 a year thereafter, would hire a new central district administrator and four full-time assistants who would coordinate each school's anti-dating-violence programs and would train a teacher or staff member on each campus to "help students identify when they may be veering toward physical, emotional, or verbal abuse and to raise awareness of these issues."

Questioning Dysfunctional Schools

Zimmer got a boost for his effort in late September when an 18-year-old student, Abraham Lopez, fatally stabbed his 17-year-old ex-girlfriend, Cindi Santana, during lunch at South East High School. If any politician were inclined to oppose Zimmer's proposal, it will be harder to do so in the wake of the Santana stabbing. Nevertheless, a few questions about this symbol of our dysfunctional schools present themselves:

- Why is a school program necessary to teach students to recognize if they are in an abusive relationship? Here's a simple test: If you are being mentally or physically abused, you are in an abusive relationship.
- Why are seventh-graders dating?
- Isn't teaching about dating the family's responsibility? The all-purpose justification for the takeover of schools by the

social work bureaucracy is: "Parents are not doing their jobs." But the causality here works both ways. The more that schools purport to take on the functions of parents, the more marginalized those parents become and the less class time is devoted to the academic material that could help propel students out of underclass culture.

- How can a government employee hope to instill in a child the subtle understanding of self, usually built up over years of interactions with parents, that would insulate someone from an abusive relationship? If government social workers could stem social breakdown, inner-city family structure would be the healthiest in the world.

The School Social Work Bureaucracy

Schools have been piling on social services for decades, yet the illegitimacy rate continues to rise, most cataclysmically among blacks (73 percent) and Latinos (53 percent). (Teen birth rates have gone down since the early 1990s, though they are still magnitudes higher than in Europe and Asia.) The social dysfunction that results from this spiraling illegitimacy rate provides the pretext for further increasing the school social work bureaucracy.

Berendo Middle School, located in a gang-ridden section of south Los Angeles County, already has a robust therapeutic staff, including a coordinator of social services who "outreaches" to other social work agencies in the community. In 2006, I visited Berendo's Violence Intervention Program for children who show signs of gang involvement and their overwhelmingly single mothers. The students' siblings often came from a dizzying array of different fathers. The Violence Intervention Program's listless group therapy session did not inspire confidence that students were better off parked there than in front of a math textbook.

A Lobby Neutral on Family Values

The dominant ethos of the social service lobby guarantees that it will fail to stem family breakdown, even if it had any hope of serving as a viable surrogate for parental oversight to begin with. The lobby is obsessively value-neutral about promiscuity and family structure. It's fine for teens to have sex, so long as they do so in a nonsexist, non-heteronormative, condom-using way. It's also fine for women and girls to have children out of wedlock; to suggest otherwise violates the first principle of feminism: "Strong women can do it all." Children don't need fathers; they just need good "support systems."

Of course, the mainstream media and large swaths of the opinion elite are just as nonjudgmental about premature sexual activity and the disappearance of marriage as the social work bureaucracy is. The *Los Angeles Times* presented Jessica Contreras, an 18-year-old graduate of the Los Angeles Unified School District, as an example of the benefits of anti-dating-violence programs. Contreras says "she wished she had learned more about healthy relationships before she ended up in an abusive one," according to the *Times*. (Parental guidance? Not on the radar screen.) When Contreras was 14, her 18-year-old boyfriend slapped her after she "told him off" for hanging out with another girl at school. For a year afterwards, she said, "I didn't know what to think or how to feel." Jessica's bewilderment did not last long: Now 18, she is "raising her one-year-old son from another relationship." The news gets even better: "With counseling and help from programs like Peace Over Violence, she said, she knows how to define boundaries in a relationship and stand up for herself."

Apparently those "boundaries" kick in *after* granting access to private parts, not before.

The problems purportedly addressed by school social programs are unquestionably serious. The demise of the norm of sexual modesty has resulted in a grotesquely sexualized culture that many parents do nothing to counter and that the entertainment and consumer industries do everything to accentuate. Dating violence and domestic violence are likely to worsen with the growing Hispanic population, which is already responsible for large increases in domestic violence calls in big-city police departments.

Increasing Self-discipline and Academic Standards

Schools do have one powerful tool to stem this tide of dysfunction, however: homework. Asian teen pregnancy rates are negligible in part because the Asian family is still strong, but also because the children are studying so single-mindedly that they don't have time to hang out at the mall, get drunk, and fornicate.

Every school with a teen pregnancy problem should double its academic requirements and enforce consequences for blowing them off. The $2 million that Los Angeles Unified board member Steve Zimmer wants to spend on a new bureaucracy could instead be used to send the message that school is about gaining precious knowledge of the world; the money could restore lost library hours and stock library shelves with [authors Edgar Allan] Poe, [Arthur] Conan Doyle, and books conveying the excitement of science and history.

Schools have a second line of defense against social breakdown when families fail to civilize their children: a pervasive ethic of self-discipline and respect for others. Rather than creating specialized classes in various dysfunctions, schools should simply insist on nonnegotiable norms of promptness, neatness, effort, and courtesy. The KIPP schools—high-achieving, inner-city charters whose students sign enforceable pledges to behave responsibly, including following their teacher's directions—are the best examples of this civilizing environment. Students who are taught to respond respectfully to adults are less likely to abuse each other. But such traditional methods of socialization do not add to school district and union payrolls or to their supporters' electoral prospects.

Periodical and Internet Sources Bibliography

The following articles have been chosen to supplement the diverse views presented in this chapter.

Sakeena Abdulraheem	"Teen Dating Violence in the Muslim Community: Protecting the Family, Eradicating Hopelessness, and Healing the Community," Faith Trust Institute, 2010. www.faithtrustinstitute.org.
Lara Alspaugh	"Teen Dating Violence," July 16, 2009. www.livestrong.com.
Centers for Disease Control and Prevention	"Understanding Teen Dating Violence Fact Sheet," 2010. www.cdc.gov/violenceprevention.
James Cummings	"What's Behind Teen Dating Violence?," *Dayton Daily News*, September 11, 2009.
Claire Burke Draucker and Donna Martsolf	"The Role of Electronic Communication Technology in Adolescent Dating Violence," *Journal of Child and Adolescent Psychiatric Nursing*, vol. 23, no. 3, August 2010.
Judith W. Herrman	"There's a Fine Line: Adolescent Dating Violence and Prevention," *Pediatric Nursing*, vol. 35, no. 3, May–June 2009.
Gail Hornor	"Teen Dating Violence," *On the Edge*, vol. 17, no. 1, Spring 2011.
Mike Males	"Wildly Overhyped 'Tween Dating Abuse' Survey Recycled to Promote Fashion Designer's Products and Program," YouthFacts.org, January 13, 2011.
Priscilla Offenhauer and Alice R. Buchalter	"Teen Dating Violence: A Literature Review and Annotated Bibliography," National Institute of Justice, April 2011.
Carol Veravanich	"Tools to Fight Teen Dating Violence," *Orange County Register*, March 3, 2010.

OPPOSING
VIEWPOINTS®
SERIES

CHAPTER 2

What Issues Surround Teen Sex?

Chapter Preface

Although statistics provided by the Centers for Disease Control and Prevention (CDC) report that teens engage in less sexual activity, have fewer abortions, and use more contraception than in previous decades, the public perception that teen sex is an epidemic problem persists. The number of teen pregnancies has steadily declined, however, with only brief unexplained spikes since its peak in 1957, when there were 96.3 births per 1,000 teens. Moreover, many teen mothers are eighteen or nineteen years old, which in many states makes them adults. Thus, one of several controversies surrounding teen sex is why, despite these facts, public misperceptions about teen sex remain so persistent.

According to some analysts, public perceptions about teen sex changed at the same time attitudes toward marriage began to change. These commentators claim that fears of a teen sex epidemic come not from the fear that more teens are having sex but that they are having sex and not getting married. According to University of Pennsylvania sociology professor Frank Furstenberg, "It's not like people in their teens didn't have sex all along."[1] He explains, however, that in the 1950s teens who got pregnant got married. Starting in the 1960s, pregnant teens were having babies without getting married. Moreover, people were delaying marriage into their twenties. According to Columbia University School of Public Health professors John S. Santelli and Andrea J. Melnikas, "Sexual initiation is almost always non-marital today; likewise, teen child rearing has become predominantly non-marital."[2] This change in attitudes toward the relationship among sex, pregnancy, and marriage also changed how society viewed teen sex.

As a result of warring attitudes toward premarital sex, some analysts assert that both liberals and social conservatives fostered the public perception of a teen sex epidemic to promote sex education policies that supported their contrasting views. Liberals and progressives support comprehensive sex education that teaches teens about contraception and safe sex in order to reduce teen pregnancy and sexually transmitted diseases. When statistics show that most Americans have premarital sex, to focus only on abstinence is inappropriate and ineffective, they claim. Former congressman Shays Conn asserts, "Sometimes I think we are trying to repeal the law of gravity"[3] by urging all young people to remain abstinent. "There are natural instincts that young people have, and they are educated by their parents about values, and good behavior, which is good, but they also need information since some do not know that oral sex can transmit disease,"[4] he concludes. Social conservatives believe that sex outside of marriage is morally wrong and thus want to teach teens to be abstinent. Those who support abstinence-only education programs often maintain that liberals do not want to reduce teen pregnancy or prevent sexually transmitted diseases. Instead, some abstinence advocates argue that the goal of liberals is to reject the institution of marriage. According to congressman Mark Souder, "We ought not to be persuaded by these groups who, although adopting the language of science and reason . . . are really just evangelists of a . . . tragically incorrect moral vision."[5]

Clearly, the debates surrounding teen sex are hotly contested and fueled by clashing values. The authors in the follow chapter explore similar concerns in answer to the question, what issues surround teen sex? For those hoping to address the needs of teens, the question of whether false perceptions or realities will guide the debate remains to be seen.

Notes

1. Quoted in Marcia Clemmitt, "Teen Pregnancy," *CQ Researcher*, March 26, 2010.
2. John S. Santelli and Andrea J. Melnikas, "Teen Fertility in Transition: Recent and Historical Trends in the United States," *Annual Review of Public Health 2010*, December 9, 2009.
3. Quoted in "Hearing on Domestic Abstinence-Only Programs: Assessing the Evidence," House Committee on Oversight and Government Reform, April 23, 2008.

4. Quoted in "Hearing on Domestic Abstinence-Only Programs," House Committee on Oversight.
5. Quoted in "Hearing on Domestic Abstinence-Only Programs," House Committee on Oversight.

> "While the risks of disease are towering,
> we can't ignore emotional dangers—
> and the need to reintroduce the
> gravitas that comes with sex connected
> to mature, abiding love."

Early Teen Sex Is Common and Poses Serious Risks

Bernadine Healy

More than three quarters of children have had sex by the end of their teen years, maintains the author of the following viewpoint. Teaching teens that unprotected sex can lead to devastating sexually transmitted disease and unplanned pregnancy is therefore important, she asserts. What is troubling, however, is that many teens do not take sex seriously, the author argues. Thus, she reasons, in addition to teaching children about the physical dangers of early sex, parents should have conversations with their teens about the connection between sex and love and character traits such as empathy and sincerity. Bernadine Healy was an American physician and cardiologist who once headed the National Institutes of Health.

As you read, consider the following questions:

1. What does Healy say is missing in the sex education debate?
2. What examples does the author give of the sophistication of teen sex?
3. How do the brains of teen boys and girls differ, in the author's view?

Helping our kids develop into smart, tender, sexual beings is vital to their future happiness and as challenging as parenting gets. The perplexity of sex is that it's so compelling, such a power for good—and yet so dangerous for young people if they set off on the wrong track. Sex education in schools is beset with endless debate about abstinence only versus safe sex. What's missing and sorely needed is a focus on love and ennobling sexual intimacy as immutable currents in human life. Both as doctor and mother, I can't help but believe that our anything-goes society, in which impulses are immediately satisfied and sex is divorced from love and bonding, is simply not healthy physically, emotionally, or spiritually.

The Dangers of Teen Sex

If we look at what today's teens are doing, it is enough to make parents weep and safe-sex educators recognize a need greater than condoms. The Guttmacher Institute reported recently that more than 75 percent of teens have had sex by the time they are 19 years old. And sophisticated sex at that: Some 25 percent of virgins over 15 have had oral sex; of those who've had intercourse, almost all have also engaged in oral sex and 11 percent in anal sex. Of kids under 15, about 14 percent have had sexual intercourse, and a quarter of teenagers have had at least one sexually transmitted disease [STD]. In fact, young people account for half of the 19 million new STD cases each year. Safe-sex slip-ups occur even if kids know the drill, and teens are simply clueless about condom use during nonvaginal sex.

While the risks of disease are towering, we can't ignore emotional dangers—and the need to reintroduce the gravitas that comes with sex connected to mature, abiding love. (Granted, this can be tough in a teen media culture brimming with physical encounters that are casual and crudely comic.) How hard it must be to form meaningful connections when casual hookups squeeze out good old dating, and "friends with benefits" becomes a new species of social relationship. The love that moves mountains and makes the world go round is something quite different, based on respecting and cherishing if not adoring another human being for his or her worth, in the sparkle of romance and affection. And I'll go out on a limb and say that this is what most young people still dream of, girls and boys alike.

One message for those intimate parent-child conversations is that early sex is a threat, and it remains a greater threat to girls than to boys. Teen pregnancy occurs in about 750,000 girls each year. Compared with adults, a teen, with an immature cervix, is more likely to catch an STD, triggering problems like smoldering pelvic inflammatory disease that can silently take away fertility, tubal pregnancies, cervical and even throat cancer, and transmission of disease to offspring at birth. That doesn't mean boys are invulnerable; they just suffer fewer and milder consequences.

A Lack of Emotional Development

However much our daughters should take equality with men for granted, they must know that sex is distinctly sexist. An old saying goes that men give love to get sex while women have sex to get love. There's something there. The brains of teen boys are raging with the libido hormone testosterone, while girls have some increase in testosterone but at far lower levels. In contrast, girls have more oxytocin, the cuddle hormone, and seem to be more sensitive to it than boys. Also, teenage emotions are responding to basic instincts from the lower brain, which awakens the body to its generative capacities. Such impulses searching for instant

Young Adults and Sexually Transmitted Infections

- Young people aged 13–24 made up about 17% of all people diagnosed with HIV/AIDS in the United States in 2008.
- Although 15–24-year-olds represent only one-quarter of the sexually active population, they account for nearly half (9.1 million) of the 18.9 million new cases of STIs [sexually transmitted infections] each year.
- Human papillomavirus (HPV) infections account for about half of STIs diagnosed among 15–24-year-olds each year. HPV is extremely common, often asymptomatic and generally harmless. However, certain types . . . can lead to cervical cancer.

Guttmacher Institute, "Facts on American Teens' Sexual and Reproductive Health," February 2012. www.guttmacher.org.

gratification can easily overwhelm the higher frontal lobes—which impose thoughtful, rational, and conscience-driven restraints on behavior—because, by some quirk of nature, those distinctly human higher cognitive centers don't fully mature until the early 20s. Parents, like it or not, have no choice but to be their kids' frontal lobes for a time, and that's a source of vintage teen turbulence.

Parents are here to help their kids, each with his or her unique temperament, fulfill their dreams. And dreams of enduring love, encouraged, prepared for, and taken seriously, prompt wiser choices in general and nourish qualities like empathy, sincerity, and human closeness. It's not all sex talk; it's serious life talk, though it comes with the frustration of not quite knowing if—hello—anyone is listening. Be patient. This past spring, I opened a Mother's Day card from our 28-year-old, just married daughter, embossed with just three words: "You were right." Music to any mom's heart.

"The reality is that in many ways, today's teenagers are more conservative about sex than previous generations."

Most Teens Are Not Engaging In Risky Sexual Behavior

Tara Parker-Pope

Despite public perceptions that more teens are engaging in risky sexual behavior at ever-younger ages, studies show that the opposite is true, argues the author of the following viewpoint. One explanation for this misperception is that the nature of dating has changed: casual gatherings of teens have replaced the traditional dating pair, she asserts. Moreover, a more relaxed attitude to oral sex among adults explains the rise in oral sex among teens, the author claims. Because teen sex requires a lack of supervision, changes in their environment say more about teen sex than a change in teen attitudes, she maintains. Tara Parker-Pope writes a weekly consumer health column and daily health blog for the New York Times.

As you read, consider the following questions:

1. According to Parker-Pope, when did the pattern shift from the planned and structured dating relationship to the casual gathering of teens?

2. What does the author claim likely explains the recent rise in teenage pregnancy rates?

3. Why does Dr. Kathleen Bogle believe that it is so difficult to convince people that teens are not out of control, in the author's view?

H ave American teenagers gone wild?
Parents have worried for generations about changing moral values and risky behavior among young people, and the latest news seems particularly worrisome.

It came from the National Center for Health Statistics, which reported this month [January 2009] that births to 15- to 19-year-olds had risen for the first time in more than a decade.

And that is not the only alarm being sounded. The talk show host Tyra Banks declared a teen sex crisis last fall after her show surveyed girls about sexual behavior. A few years ago, Oprah Winfrey warned parents of a teenage oral-sex epidemic.

Misleading News Distorts Reality

The news is troubling, but it's also misleading. While some young people are clearly engaging in risky sexual behavior, a vast majority are not. The reality is that in many ways, today's teenagers are more conservative about sex than previous generations.

Today, fewer than half of all high school students have had sex: 47.8 percent as of 2007, according to the National Youth Risk Behavior Survey, down from 54.1 percent in 1991.

A less recent report suggests that teenagers are also waiting longer to have sex than they did in the past. A 2002 report from the Department of Health and Human Services found that 30 percent of 15- to 17-year-old girls had experienced sex, down from 38 percent in 1995. During the same period, the percentage of sexually experienced boys in that age group dropped to 31 percent from 43 percent.

Trends in the Prevalence of Sexual Behaviors

This table shows the percentage of surveyed students in ninth through twelfth grades in public and private schools throughout the United States.

	1991	2001	2005	2009	Change from 1991–2009
Ever had sexual intercourse	54.1%	45.6 %	46.8%	46.0%	Decreased
Used a condom during last sexual intercourse	46.2%	57.9 %	62.8%	61.1%	Increased 1991–2003 No change 2003–2009
Drank alcohol or used drugs before last sexual intercourse	21.6%	25.6%	23.3%	21.6%	Increased 1991–2001 Decreased 2001–2009

TAKEN FROM: US Department of Health and Human Services, Centers for Disease Control and Prevention, Youth Risk Behavior Survey, 1991–2009.

The rates also went down among younger teenagers. In 1995, about 20 percent said they had had sex before age 15, but by 2002 those numbers had dropped to 13 percent of girls and 15 percent of boys.

"There's no doubt that the public perception is that things are getting worse, and that kids are having sex younger and are much wilder than they ever were," said Kathleen A. Bogle, an assistant professor of sociology and criminal justice at La Salle University. "But when you look at the data, that's not the case."

A Changing Dating Pattern

One reason people misconstrue teenage sexual behavior is that the system of dating and relationships has changed significantly.

In the first half of the 20th century, dating was planned and structured—and a date might or might not lead to a physical relationship. In recent decades, that pattern has largely been replaced by casual gatherings of teenagers.

In that setting, teenagers often say they "fool around," and in a reversal of the old pattern, such an encounter may or may not lead to regular dating. The shift began around the late 1960s, said Dr. Bogle, who explored the trend in her book *Hooking Up: Sex, Dating and Relationships on Campus*.

The latest rise in teenage pregnancy rates is cause for concern. But it very likely reflects changing patterns in contraceptive use rather than a major change in sexual behavior. The reality is that the rate of teenage childbearing has fallen steeply since the late 1950s. The declines aren't explained by the increasing availability of abortions: teenage abortion rates have also dropped.

"There is a group of kids who engage in sexual behavior, but it's not really significantly different than previous generations," said Maria Kefalas, an associate professor of sociology at St. Joseph's University in Philadelphia and co-author of *Promises I Can Keep: Why Poor Women Put Motherhood Before Marriage*. "This creeping up of teen pregnancy is not because so many more kids are having sex, but most likely because more kids aren't using contraception."

As for that supposed epidemic of oral sex, especially among younger teenagers: national statistics on the behavior have only recently been collected, and they are not as alarming as some reports would have you believe. About 16 percent of teenagers say they have had oral sex but haven't yet had intercourse. Researchers say children's more relaxed attitude about oral sex probably reflects a similar change among adults since the 1950s. In addition, some teenagers may view oral sex as "safer," since unplanned pregnancy is not an issue.

Looking at the Wrong Problem

Health researchers say parents who fret about teenage sex often fail to focus on the important lessons they can learn from the kids who aren't having sex. Teenagers with more parental supervision, who come from two-parent households and who are doing well in school are more likely to delay sex until their late teens or beyond.

"For teens, sex requires time and lack of supervision," Dr. Kefalas said. "What's really important for us to pay attention to, as researchers and as parents, are the characteristics of the kids who become pregnant and those who get sexually transmitted diseases.

"This whole moral panic thing misses the point, because research suggests kids who don't use contraception tend to be kids who are feeling lost and disconnected and not doing well."

Although the data is clear, health researchers say it is often hard to convince adults that most teenagers have healthy attitudes about sex.

"I give presentations nationwide where I'm showing people that the virginity rate in college is higher than you think and the number of partners is lower than you think and hooking up more often than not does not mean intercourse," Dr. Bogle said. "But so many people think we're morally in trouble, in a downward spiral and teens are out of control. It's very difficult to convince people otherwise."

*"Children . . . are the ones who
are unprepared to deal with the
consequences of their sexual behavior."*

Dating Teens Should Not Have Sex

Armstrong Williams

*Teens are not ready to handle the consequences and therefore
should not have sex, claims the author of the following viewpoint.
Despite sex education and widely available birth control options,
the rates of teen pregnancy, abortion, and sexually transmitted diseases in the United States are the highest in the Western world, he
maintains. Because these programs have failed, parents must do
whatever it takes to prevent their children from having sex, the
author reasons. Schools, media, and lawmakers must support parents' efforts, he concludes. Armstrong Williams is the author of a
conservative newspaper column, the host of a daily radio show,
and a nationally syndicated TV program.*

As you read, consider the following questions:

1. According to an Associated Press poll, what percentage of
   American adults favor providing birth control to students
   in public schools?

2. How does the author say his parents prevented him from having sex as a teenager?

3. Why does the author claim that schools, churches, media, and lawmakers must support parents in their efforts to prevent their teens from having sex?

Recently a study was released by Paige Harden, a doctoral candidate in psychology at the University of Virginia, that claimed teenagers or pre-teens who have consensual sex are less likely than their virgin counterparts to engage in delinquent behavior later on in life. Then, last week [December 2007] I read about an author who was telling parents to encourage their youngsters to engage in sexual activity. And to top it off, just the other day I read about the results of a recent Associated Press poll which showed that 67 percent of American adults favor public schools providing birth control to students. All this after the nation's teen birth rate rose 3 percent from 2005 to 2006, which was the first increase in 14 years and births to unmarried mothers hit a record high (Centers for Disease Control [and Prevention]).

Unprepared for the Consequences

What is our society coming to when we encourage our children to have sex, when we hand out condoms in classrooms, and when we claim that teenage sex is actually beneficial? Are you kidding me here? Is this a joke of some sort? Whether you have kids or not, you should have learned enough from your own experiences to know that pre-marital sex (and especially teenage sex) is not something to mess around with. From unwanted pregnancies to sexually transmitted diseases [STDs], sex can cause a world of hurt for those who are unprepared for the consequences. And 99 percent of the time, it is our children who are the ones who are unprepared to deal with the consequences of their sexual behavior. Are they ready to drop out of school and go to work to support a child? Of course not! Are they prepared to find an abortion clinic or adoption center and figure out their options? Doubtful! Are they prepared to go through nine months of pregnancy and all the strains that are brought about? Absolutely not! And are they prepared to raise a child when they themselves are not even old enough to drive or vote? The answer is as clear as day: NO.

Despite recent decreases, American rates of teen pregnancy, childbirth, abortion, and sexually transmitted diseases are among the highest of all industrialized nations (*Washington Post*, 2006). This shows me that despite our quality education system, despite our efforts to provide sexual education programs, and despite the barrage of birth control options, American teenagers are having sex and paying the consequences. One study estimated that the average American loses their virginity at the age of 16. Another claimed that less than 30 percent of American teenagers graduate high school a virgin. These alarming statistics, and the sorrow that sex can bring to youngsters, leads me to believe that parents aren't doing their job—or at least not well enough.

Taking Strong Steps to Prevent Sex

My parents knew my brothers, sisters, and I would be tempted by sex as teenagers so they took specific, consistent, and sometimes dramatic steps to prevent it from happening. They demanded we participate in extra curricular activities to keep us busy. They enforced a strict curfew and delivered consequences should we arrive home late. They called our friends' parents if we asked to attend a party or sleep-over. They even barred me from having a girl in my bedroom, even to study! My parents took a hands-on approach to parenting and their demands and discipline kept my siblings and me in line.

Too often today I hear about parents who are too busy, distracted, or tired to get involved in their child's lives. I hear about parents who work two jobs, or houses where kids have the home to themselves from the minute they get home from school until the minute they go to sleep. What do you think these kids are doing? Their homework? Of course not. These children, with time on their hands, no supervision, and little structure in their lives, are getting themselves into trouble. Whether it is drinking, drugs, or sex, I promise you, it's not good.

Parents must not only discourage their children from engaging in sexual activity, they must demand it, and, like my parents, take steps to prevent it. Kids without this parental support will fall to temptation, follow the path of their peers, and engage in sexual behavior that could lead to pregnancy, abortion, an STD, or simply, heartache, depression, or dejection. Then it is up to our schools, churches, media, and lawmakers to support parents so that parents are not alone in keeping their children safe, healthy, and out of bed. And finally, it is up to the child themselves to head the advice of their elders, take the right path, and avoid pre-marital sex.

The reward does not outweigh the risk. The thrill of sex lasts a few minutes, hours, or days, but the consequences that could—and most likely will—arise can last a lifetime.

"*The peer group provides checks and balances . . . about what's OK and what's not, so kids are less likely to get out of their depth—especially in terms of conflict, expectations for behaviour and sex.*"

New Teen Dating Practices Reduce the Likelihood of Sex

Marcia Kaye

Today's dating world has changed significantly, maintains the author of the following viewpoint. This new pattern of group dating actually reduces the risks that accompany more intimate dating relationships because having friends nearby encourages appropriate behavior, she asserts. Although dating groups are getting younger, most intimate relationships end quickly, the author claims. Sex does not play a significant role in these relationships, she suggests. In fact, she argues, studies show a drop in the number of teens having sex. Marcia Kaye is a Canadian health research journalist and a contributing author to the trilogy Growing with Your Child, Raising Great Kids, *and* Understanding Your Teen.

As you read, consider the following questions:

1. What do experts such as psychologist Jennifer Connolly say is healthy and positive about having friendships between boys and girls at a young age, according to Kaye?

2. What do the author and sexual health educator Kim Martyn say are the risks of teens flirting with bisexuality?

3. What does the author claim is the attitude among teens toward marriage?

Here is how 14-year-old Catherine started going out with the guy who is now her boyfriend. At recess one day, her best friend yelled over to the unsuspecting boy, "Catherine wants to snog!" Everyone within earshot knew from Harry Potter that "snog" is Brit[ish] slang for "kiss." While Catherine and her friends dissolved into hysterics, the boy didn't react at all—until two weeks later, when he approached Catherine to ask her out. And here's how that went:

Boy: "Do you wanna go out?"

Catherine: "OK."

The two Toronto-area teens have been going out since last April [2008], although rarely on their own. In their group of eight friends, the four boys and four girls are paired off into couples, but prefer to spend their time all together, sitting around and talking at one another's houses, grabbing something to eat, going to a movie. So why bother having a boyfriend at all? "We just feel better when we're together," Catherine explains. "At this age we're always fighting with our parents, so we need to feel we're loved." She's quick to add that while she and her boyfriend love each other, they're not in love. "Whoa—we're only 14!"

This is the new world of teen dating, and it can be almost unrecognizable to many parents. Long gone is the tradition where a boy phones a girl on Tuesday to ask her out for Saturday, picks her up at her house, meets the parents, pays for dinner and a show, and sees her home. "That's just in the movies," says Brett,

14, of Aurora [Ontario, Canada]. "What happens in real life is you'll be hanging out with your immediate circle of friends, including your girlfriend, and you go, 'What's everybody doing Friday night?' You all decide to see a movie and you'll all get separate drives there. You usually don't go out one-on-one."

And there are some other interesting developments in this brave new world, including the fact that teens feel freer to put off sex, and they see love, marriage and kids as best left for the (fairly) distant future. Here's our look at teen dating in the 21st century.

The Gang's All Here

Going out with your significant other with all your mutual friends in tow is such a common phenomenon across the country that academics have started researching it. "We call it group dating, and we believe it can be really healthy and protective," says Jennifer Connolly, a psychology professor at York University in Toronto who specializes in teen relationships. Connolly, who has two adolescent daughters of her own, says that group dating is growing in popularity everywhere, including China and India. The peer group provides checks and balances, along with feedback about what's OK and what's not, so kids are less likely to get out of their depth—especially in terms of conflict, expectations for behaviour and sex.

With traditional one-to-one relationships, Connolly says, things tend to escalate much more quickly, simply because the couple is spending a lot of time alone. Having supportive friends around can exert a powerful moderating influence. But by the same token, a tough, aggressive peer group can have a negative influence, such as tolerating dating violence. "So from a parenting perspective," says Connolly, who is also the director of the LaMarsh Centre for Research on Violence and Conflict Resolution, "you want to know who your kids are friends with."

Kids like the security of having their friends around. "When you're going out with someone, it's much easier to be yourself when your friends are there too," says Katie, 15, of Carleton

Place, Ont. "If you pretended to be somebody else, your friends would go, 'Whoa, why are you acting so weird?'" Also, there's no need to pre-arrange that cellphone call to get you out of a date you're not enjoying. "If I get bored [on a date], my friends keep things interesting," Katie says.

The downside for parents: You may not even be aware that your child has a boyfriend or girlfriend. Group dating is also a way for kids to circumvent a parental ban on dating.

Becoming a "Couple"

Don't panic, but the experts say "going out" often begins in grade five, with one or two couples in a class. A couple may never see or speak to each other outside of school, although they may well enjoy the new status accorded them by their peers. These types of short-lived pairings—relationships in name only—jump in numbers by grades six and seven, when alcohol increasingly becomes part of many parties. "This 'liquid courage,' which is far more common than other drugs, makes kids get over their natural modesty and social awkwardness," says Kim Martyn, a long-time sexual health educator in Toronto. Parents must acknowledge this reality and address safety issues around the risks of drinking, says Martyn, who's also the mother of two young-adult daughters. But, she adds reassuringly, many of these youthful relationships, sustained largely by rumour and reputation, will have dissolved within days or weeks.

Regardless, there are still many, many kids who haven't the slightest interest in going out. Eleven-year-old Charles, a bright, sociable, engaging sixth-grader in the Toronto area, was shocked to hear last spring that a buddy's school in a nearby town would be hosting a grade-five dance. "I think that's just ridiculous," says Charles, who doesn't feel ready for that kind of intimacy with girls. "I just spent the weekend at my grandparents' place moving rocks. That's my idea of fun."

There's certainly been an increase in boy-girl parties at younger ages, including mixed sleepovers. This causes parents to worry, and rightly so, as many kids are uncomfortable with or unable to handle the intimacy that comes with slow dancing or mixed-gender pyjama parties. But in terms of friendships between boys and girls, Connolly says that simply having friends of both sexes can be healthy and positive. And for some kids, it may even help to ease the pressure to get involved in one-to-one dating before they're ready.

Despite texting, email and instant messaging, most relationships still begin face-to-face. "It's more intellectually stimulating to talk to someone in person or even on the phone," says Kim, an 18-year-old who lives north of Toronto. "When you just type something, the emotion and the subtleties aren't there." All the kids in this article said they're on the computer far less than they used to be.

Flirting with Bisexuality

Martyn sees another trend: kids, especially girls between ages 13 and 15, flirting around the edges of bisexuality. "Girl-on-girl make-outs are somewhat fashionable, but it's a bit of a performance thing," she says. "There's some kissing, maybe some slow dancing at a party, and a lot of talk, usually in front of friends. They want to be outrageous, and they know it gets guys' attention."

But this behaviour is more a reflection of our culture, drenched as it is in sexual imagery, than of freedom for gay kids to come out. Although people who are gay typically don't define their sexual identity until their late teens, or 20s, Martyn says that a young person questioning his or her sexual orientation could become very confused seeing such same-sex play-acting among their friends. The good news, though, is that spending time with friends of both sexes could help a gay youth resolve important identity questions over the next several years.

Codes of Conduct

With so much pushing of the envelope, it may seem that there are no rules around relationships. But there are. "Relationships are very rule-bound, and kids absolutely understand this," says Connolly. "It's only as they get older that they feel they can go beyond the rules and become an individual."

The rules can vary from group to group, but here are some common ones:

- No making out in public. Holding hands or a light kiss is fine, but nothing sloppy or groping. "It's considered taboo—we don't need to see that!" says Katie. Catherine was appalled last year, in grade eight, to learn of a couple who got caught making out on school property by a lunch monitor. "There were itty-bitty grade-oners running around!" Catherine says in horror. "It was like, 'Eww!' Pretty nasty."

- Girls can do the asking, but guys have the final say. "It's not considered weird for a girl to ask a guy out," Katie says. But 13-year-old Anthony says it's usually still the guy who makes the first move. When asked why that is, Anthony replies, "The guy's supposed to be the stronger person, the tough one." Connolly says: "Girls are fine today to be or-chestrators of group dating, but when it comes to announc-ing 'We're a couple,' the responsibility still falls to the boys."

- No cheating. If you're going out with someone, you can't go out or make out with anyone else until you officially break up with the first person. This applies to boys as well as girls, which means the once-cool image of male "studs" and "players" is now just as scorned as female "sluts." Brett explains, "If a guy's going out with a lot of girls, people will look at him and go, 'You tool, what are you doing?' It low-ers your status."

How Do I Love Thee?

Catherine was recently stunned to hear that her 12-year-old cousin in Edmonton is in love with her boyfriend. But, Martyn says, "love can be as real for a 12-year-old as for a 30-year-old.

The Language of Love

Not only is the concept of dating antiquated, but the very word "date" is, well, dated. Here's a glossary of the latest lingo:

Going Out: Publicly acknowledging that you like someone and he or she likes you. The two of you don't have to technically go out at all, but you'll likely sit together at lunch, walk home together or spend a little more time texting or talking. All your friends will know that the two of you are going out.

Making Out: Also previously known as necking, petting, fooling around or getting to first (or second) base. (All these expressions are eye-rollingly archaic to kids today.)

Hooking Up: This gets tricky. It means physical intimacy between two people who normally aren't going out, but it can cover everything from kissing to sex. Explains 15-year-old Katie, "In grade nine it means kissing, in grade 10 it means something more intense, and in grades 11 and 12 it can mean sexual relations or just holding hands. If I hear that two people hooked up, usually I have to ask, 'In what way exactly did they hook up?'"

PDAs: Public displays of affection.

Friends with Benefits: Two people who meet solely for casual sex. Also called sex buddies (and other more graphic terms). This arrangement is rare among younger teens.

Marcia Kaye, "Modern Love," Today's
Parent, *vol. 26, no. 2, February 2009.*

We certainly bought it with Romeo and Juliet, and she was only 13!" Martyn says it's not helpful for parents to dismiss their son's or daughter's strong emotional attachment as infatuation, puppy love or a crush.

Connolly agrees: "Of course kids can be in love. They're capable of having very strong, loving relationships that connect companionship and emotional intimacy with sexuality," But what these relationships lack is longevity. Connolly says that young adolescent relationships last from a few weeks to a year, with the average being four months. While some are extremely intense, others remain very casual. "Love is a strong word," says Brett. "Mostly we just say, 'I like this person.'" But adolescents all understand the distinction between "like" and "like like."

The Role of Sex

And despite our sex-saturated culture, sex is usually not a big part of young relationships. A Statistics Canada study published in August 2008 found that only 43 percent of teens aged 15 to 19 reported in 2005 that they'd had sexual intercourse at least once, a drop from 47 percent in 1996/97. Only eight percent reported having sex before age 15, down from the previous 12 percent. And the latest teen pregnancy figures show a steady drop over the past couple of decades, especially among girls aged 15 to 17, according to the latest figures from SIECCAN, the Sex Information and Education Council of Canada. It's almost counterintuitive, but it appears that the more kids know about sex, the less likely they are to actually have it. "Canadian society has become increasingly accepting of the reality of adolescent sexuality, which has made discussions much more open," says Alex McKay, SIECCAN's research coordinator. "Young people feel much more free to seek information, and that has empowered increasing numbers of youth to find they're not ready for early sexual activity."

Intimacy in young relationships is often limited to hugging, kissing, holding hands and the comfort of knowing that though you often feel at odds with your parents, your teachers and the world, there's somebody who likes you just as you are. Catherine says, "It's nice to have a boyfriend who's the same age and has the same sense of humour—we're pretty much exactly the same."

But about a sexual relationship, she says, "We aren't even close to anything like that."

Many don't feel ready for early marriage, either. Kim says that while she loves her boyfriend of two years, she has no plans to get married in her teens, as her own mother did. "A relationship is hard enough to keep together without the whole stressful process of a wedding," she says. "I'm not even thinking of having kids yet. I need more time to grow."

Katie says that marriage was something she and her girlfriends fantasized about in elementary school, but now they see it as a possibility in the far-off future, if ever. "A lot of my friends are gay and don't necessarily expect to be married at all," Katie says. "I think it would be nice to be married and have children some day when I'm 35."

Letting Go

Since adolescent relationships are typically brief, breakups are common. Catherine broke up with her first boyfriend by approaching him at school, saying "Here!" and handing him a note that read, "I think we should break up and see other people." He agreed.

Kids might even prepare for the breakup before they start going out. Brett says, "What happens most of the time is if you're really good friends and you're both looking to go forward, you say, 'If this doesn't work out, let's still be friends and forget this ever happened.'" He adds that the typical way to break up is to say, "I liked you better when we were really good friends."

Breakups between young teens are often mutual and rarely cause a long-lasting broken heart, says Connolly. Most of the time they serve to help kids learn about themselves and how they might want to shape their future relationships.

And after the breakup, there's no pressure to jump into another relationship. In fact, it's becoming increasingly OK to not always have a boyfriend or girlfriend. "I'm 15," says Katie. "I think I'm allowed to be single from time to time!"

> "*Understandably, many teens lack the foresight, and probably the cognitive makeup, to accurately anticipate all of the possible, even predictable, results of sexual behavior.*"

Teens Who Have Sex Risk Physical and Emotional Harm

Stephen G. Wallace

The author of the following viewpoint argues that teens who have sex risk not only early pregnancy and sexually transmitted diseases but also emotional problems. Unfortunately, many teens view sex as a normal part of adolescent life, which media images reinforce, he claims. Moreover, the author maintains, some teens see sex as a recreational activity, and many feel pressured to have sex before they are ready. Regrettably, studies show that those who engage in sex as teens have higher rates of stress and depression than those who do not, he concludes. Stephen G. Wallace, a school psychologist and adolescent counselor, is a professor of psychology at Mount Ida College in Massachusetts.

As you read, consider the following questions:

1. In Wallace's opinion, what almost innate drive influences teen decision making?
2. What did a University of California, Santa Barbara, study reveal about the sexual content in television?
3. In the author's view, how do gender stereotypes hurt teens?

Reports of a fourteen-year-old middle school girl performing oral sex on a sixteen-year-old high school boy differed only slightly from scores of similar tales making headlines across the country. The setting (a school bus) and the audience (classmates) made it especially unappealing, but really not that surprising. After all, it was not long before that news broke of a senior class scavenger hunt proffering points for proof (videos and such) of masturbation and public intercourse, and not long after that a widely publicized episode of group oral sex rocked a storied New England prep school.

Such incidents in a diverse set of institutions and communities nationwide raise important questions about early intimacy among teens and the physical, social, emotional, and legal toll it can take on young lives.

Just as important, it points to a "reality gap" between increasingly normative sexual behavior among youth and commonly held perceptions of adults. Perhaps the public nature of heretofore private tales may at last awaken the sleeping giant of awareness and communication needed to keep teens safe.

During adolescence, psychology (eagerness for independence, control, and acceptance) joins with biology (hormones) in a fuse that may lead quickly to intimacy. Still-developing adolescent brains wrestling with judgment can then provide the spark. Understandably, many teens lack the foresight, and probably the cognitive makeup, to accurately anticipate all of the possible, even predictable, results of sexual behavior. This developmental disconnect accounts for all types of destructive decisions, from driving drunk to having unprotected sex. But all of that can explain the motivation behind teen sexual behavior for generations, so why the dramatic shift in adolescent attitudes lately? At least part of the answer rests with the social "norming" of teen sex and adult indifference or inattention.

Social Norming

While each of us is influenced by what we view as common and acceptable behavior, this is especially true during adolescence, when an almost innate drive to "go along to get along" can weight decision-making. After all, who doesn't want to be "normal?" Fifteen-year-old Kevin had oral sex with a girl he hardly knew because, "I thought everyone else had done it." And fourteen-year-old Jake rates feeling pressured to have sex as the single biggest source of stress in his life.

That pressure affects both sexes but seems particularly common among boys, leading to early sexual activity less because they want it and more because they believe it's time they did. Blair says, "I must be the only eighteen-year-old on the planet who hasn't had sex." Thirteen year-old Bryan says, "I just want to do it all at once and get it over with." And sixteen-year-old Connor, after exchanging genital touches with a girl following a dance, expresses relief: "I finally did it."

Media images that portray sex as casual and unimportant don't help, but only create a false sense of acceptability and urgency in the minds of those already predisposed to test limits and take risks. As one high school teen put it, "If you watch TV, you just assume everyone is having sex." Fourteen-year-old Bridget concurs, saying that the media plays a big role in teen decision-making about sex, sending the message that "Sex is good." Fifteen-year-old Scott adds, "Television, movies, and music add to the pressure of wanting to have sex. They portray how men should be masculine and hook up with women." And Robert, a college senior, recalls his race to have intercourse at age eighteen: "I didn't want to go into college being a virgin, because movies like *American Pie* made it clear you lost your virginity in high school."

In short, content equals consequence. And, sadly, there's no shortage of content. A study conducted at the University of California, Santa Barbara, found that:

- Two thirds of all television shows (64 percent) have some sexual content, including one in three (32 percent) with sexual behaviors;

- One in seven shows (14 percent) now includes sexual intercourse; and

- In the top twenty shows among teen viewers, eight in ten episodes included some sexual content (83 percent), including one in five (20 percent) with sexual intercourse.

The Reality Gap

Many adults are simply unaware of the pressures and choices young people face every day when it comes to sexual behavior. For example, compared to what their parents say about them, high school teens are twice as likely to say they have had sex. Unfortunately, not knowing about the incredibly sexualized world in which teens live impairs adults' ability to help them navigate the maze of information, influence, and decision-making.

What does that world look like? According to *Teens Today* research from SADD (Students Against Destructive Decisions), almost one in four sixth-graders and one in three seventh-graders have engaged in sexual behavior. More than three in four twelfth-graders report the same.

Hidden behind those numbers is an increasingly pervasive attitude that, at least short of intercourse, sex—if you even call it that—just doesn't matter. Seventeen-year-old Taylor says he started having genital sex with girls during freshman year before moving on to oral sex with several partners. "They were hook-up buddies. You know, just hooking up for friends. We'd meet up at parties, never strictly for sex, but both of us would know it was going to happen."

Sex with a friend, sex with a stranger, sex in private, sex in public; it all boils down to just having fun. It's no big deal.

Or is it?

A Reality Check

With sexual activity being reported by one quarter of middle school students and almost two thirds of high school students, related diseases and illnesses are catastrophic. Of the 12 million cases of STDs (or STIs) [sexually transmitted diseases or infections] diagnosed annually in the United States, about 8 million are among people under the age of twenty-five.

Others argue that the psychological outfall isn't far behind. Tellingly, many girls and boys who have been sexually active say they wish they had waited. Fifteen-year-old Stephanie explained that she began to have a physical relationship with her boyfriend, Craig, during her freshman year of high school, even though "it felt weird." But Stephanie went along anyway, and by the beginning of sophomore year she'd agreed to have intercourse. "I had always told myself I would wait until I was in love, comfortable. But Craig kept asking. Afterwards I thought, 'What did I just do? Am I out of my mind?'"

Steve, an eighteen-year-old senior, expressed sadness and disappointment at having been tricked into having sexual intercourse in the backseat of a car with a girl he had known for only two weeks. "I regret the whole experience with her. It wasn't real. Something in me knew she didn't care about me, but I tried not to listen to that, and I felt bad when I realized she was just in it for sex. In the future, I'll have to know a lot about the person, love the person. Now I know what can happen."

Seventeen-year-old Stacy figured she didn't want to take the chance. "My boyfriend wanted to but I said 'no.' I didn't want to regret the decision."

Teens Today research may tell us why many young people do regret their decisions to become sexually active. The results indicate that adolescents who engage in early sexual behavior experience higher levels of stress and depression than their non-sexually-active peers do.

Of course, it's hard to know which is the chicken and which is the egg. Young people (and adults) sometimes use sexual behavior as a form of self-medication to feel better about their lives.

The Great Debate

The incidences of, rationale for, and potential consequences related to teen sex form a backdrop against which a continuing debate about the appropriateness of such behavior continues to rage.

In her book, *The Sex Lives of Teenagers: Revealing the Secret World of Adolescent Boys and Girls*, psychiatrist Lynn Ponton makes the case that sex is a fact of life for all young adults, even if only in fantasy. Further down that path went Judith Levine in *Harmful to Minors: The Perils of Protecting Children from Sex*, essentially arguing that sex is not inherently a bad thing for teens, more so the stigmatizing of it.

Although some more conservative groups issue cautionary tales, the federal Centers for Disease Control, the National Campaign Against Teen Pregnancy, and books such as physician Meg Meeker's *Epidemic: How Teen Sex Is Killing Our Kids* focus on the public health issues posed by early and risky sexual behavior among adolescents.

Ideology and science aside, there is no question that teens live in a world different from the one most adults experienced just a generation ago.

Recreational vs. Relational Sex

Sure, sexual behavior among adolescents is nothing new. But what is new is the startling casualness and regularity with which the "hooking up" takes place. The metamorphosis from relationship-based (relational) sex to recreational sex has many experts wondering if some young people are jeopardizing their future ability to form significant emotional attachments and construct healthy adult relationships.

According to *Teens Today*, more than half of young people say their primary motivation to have intercourse or to engage in other sexual activity is to have fun (56 percent and 55 percent, respectively), while almost as many report engaging in those behaviors to feel closer to a boyfriend or girlfriend (65 percent and 61 percent, respectively).

Other changes are in the offing as well.

Gender Stereotypes

Adolescent sexual behavior has long been linked to gender stereotypes, such as ones that suggest boys want, and should seek, all the sex they can get and that girls are simply targets of turbo-charged testosterone. Both of these stereotypes hurt teens—boys because they feel pressure to be sexually active and girls because they often cannot "safely" discuss or explore their sexuality.

But the shifting culture of teen sex may soon reshape those views, although not necessarily for the better. Justin, a fourteen-year-old eighth-grader, says, "Teachers think it's the boys trying to get sex, but now it's the girls." Seventeen-year-old Neil agrees. "They're like guys now, pointing out who they had sex with: 'I did him, I did him, I did him.'" The "hunter-gatherer" subtext common in such analysis does little to adequately frame the complicated nature of sexual decision-making, by boys or girls.

Fortunately, decisions about sex are not made in a vacuum. Teens weigh all kinds of factors when making choices about personal behavior, including information and expectations communicated by the caring adults in their lives.

Unfortunately, that dialogue appears to be more the exception than the rule. A new *Teens Today* study reveals just how rare it is for adults and teens to discuss this most basic—and important—

facet of growing up: just over half of middle and high school students (51 percent) say they can talk to their parents about sex and significantly fewer cite other adults with whom they can discuss the issue (34 percent).

> "Comprehensive sex education programs . . . can help youth delay onset of sexual activity, reduce the frequency of sexual activity, reduce number of sexual partners, and increase condom and contraceptive use."

Comprehensive Sex Education Will Reduce the Risks of Teen Sex

Advocates for Youth

Comprehensive sex education programs do not increase the likelihood that teens will be more sexually active, claim the authors of the following viewpoint. In fact, they argue, the opposite is true: these programs delay teen sexual activity, and for teens who do have sex, they increase condom and contraceptive use. Furthermore, public opinion supports comprehensive sex education, while little evidence shows that abstinence programs are effective, they assert. To improve teen sexual health and reduce unintended pregnancy, policy makers should support comprehensive sex education, the authors reason. Advocates for Youth promotes efforts to help young people make informed and responsible decisions.

As you read, consider the following questions:

1. According to Advocates for Youth, how much has the federal government invested in abstinence-only education programs since 1997?
2. How many of the comprehensive sex education programs studied by the author demonstrated a statistically significant delay in the timing of first sex?
3. What did the December 2004 US House of Representatives' Committee on Government Reform report reveal about 80 percent of abstinence-only education programs?

Since 1997 the federal government has invested more than $1.5 billion dollars in abstinence-only programs—proven ineffective programs which censor or exclude important information that could help young people protect their health. In fact, until recently, programs which met a strict abstinence-only definition were the only type of sex education eligible for federal funding; no funding existed for comprehensive sex education, which stresses abstinence but also provides information about contraception and condoms.

But the [President Barack] Obama administration's proposed budget for FY10 [fiscal year 2010] removed the streams of funding for abstinence-only programs, and created funding for programs which have been *proven effective* at reducing teen pregnancy, delaying sexual activity, or increasing contraceptive use. Not surprisingly, it is comprehensive sex education programs which help youth remain healthy and avoid negative sexual health outcomes. This document explores the research around comprehensive sex education and abstinence-only programs.

Comprehensive Sex Education Has Been Proven Effective

Evaluations of comprehensive sex education programs show that these programs can help youth delay onset of sexual activity, reduce the frequency of sexual activity, reduce number of sexual partners, and increase condom and contraceptive use. Importantly, the evidence shows youth who receive comprehensive sex education are *not* more likely to become sexually active, increase sexual activity, or experience negative sexual health outcomes. Effective programs exist for youth from a variety of racial, cultural, and socioeconomic backgrounds.

Researchers studied the National Survey of Family Growth to determine the impact of sexuality education on youth sexual risk-taking for young people ages 15–19, and found that teens who received comprehensive sex education were 50 percent less likely to experience pregnancy than those who received abstinence-only education.

Researcher Douglas Kirby for the National Campaign to End Teen and Unplanned Pregnancy examined studies of prevention programs which had a strong experimental design and used appropriate analysis. Two-thirds of the 48 comprehensive sex-ed programs studied had positive effects.

- 40 percent delayed sexual initiation, reduced the number of sexual partners, or increased condom or contraceptive use.
- 30 percent reduced the frequency of sex, including a return to abstinence.
- 60 percent reduced unprotected sex.

Advocates for Youth undertook exhaustive reviews of existing programs to compile a list of programs that have been proven effective by rigorous evaluation. Twenty-six effective programs were identified, 23 of which included comprehensive sex education as at least one component of the program. The other programs were early childhood interventions. Of the 23 effective, comprehensive sex education programs:

- 14 programs demonstrated a statistically significant delay in the timing of first sex.

- 13 programs showed statistically significant declines in teen pregnancy, HIV, or other STIs [sexually transmitted infections].
- 14 programs helped sexually active youth to increase their use of condoms.
- 9 programs demonstrated success at increasing use of contraception other than condoms.
- 13 programs showed reductions in the number of sex partners and/or increased monogamy among program participants.
- 10 programs helped sexually active youth to reduce the incidence of unprotected sex.

Abstinence-Only Programs Are Ineffective

While there is ample research to prove that comprehensive sex education programs give young people the tools they need to protect themselves from negative sexual health outcomes, there is little if any evidence to show that flawed abstinence-only programs are effective—even at achieving abstinence among teens.

- A congressionally mandated study of four popular abstinence-only programs by the Mathematica found that they were entirely ineffective. Students who participated in the programs were no more likely to abstain from sex than other students.
- Evaluations of publicly funded abstinence-only programs in at least 13 states have shown no positive changes in sexual behaviors over time.
- In December 2004, the U.S. House of Representatives Committee on Government Reform led by Rep. Henry A. Waxman released a report showing that 80 percent of the most popular federally funded abstinence-only education programs use curricula that distort information about the

Abstinence-Only Education Cartoon. © Copyright 2008, by Jimmy Margulies and Cagle Cartoons.com.

effectiveness of contraceptives, misrepresent the risks of abortion, blur religion and science, treat stereotypes about girls and boys as scientific fact, and contain basic scientific errors.

• Among youth participating in "virginity pledge" programs, researchers found among sexually experienced youth who were re-pledging abstinence, 88 percent broke the pledge and had sex before marriage. Further, among all participants, once pledgers began to have sex, they had more partners in a shorter period of time and were less likely to use contraception or condoms than were their nonpledging peers.

• No abstinence-only program has yet been proven through rigorous evaluation to help youth delay sex for a significant period of time, help youth decrease their number of sex partners, or reduce STI or pregnancy rates among teens.

Public opinion polls consistently show that more than 80 percent of Americans support teaching comprehensive sex education in high schools and in middle or junior high schools. In one poll, 85 percent believed that teens should be taught about birth control and preventing pregnancy; in another, seven in 10 opposed government funding for abstinence-only programs. Support for comprehensive sex education also cuts across party lines. In a poll of 1,000 self-identified Republicans and Independents, 60 percent of Republicans and 81 percent of Independents think that public schools should teach comprehensive sex education.

Young People Need Comprehensive Sex Education

The health and future of every adolescent is shadowed by risk of sexually transmitted infections (STIs), including HIV, as well as by risk of involvement in unintended pregnancy.

- The rate of STIs is high among young people in the United States. Young people ages 15–24 contract almost half the nation's 19 million new STIs every year; and the CDC [Centers for Disease Control and Prevention] estimates that one in four young women ages 15–19 has an STI.

- Experts estimate that about one young person in the United States is infected with HIV *every hour of every day*.

- Nearly 15 percent of the 56,000 annual new cases of HIV infections in the United States occurred in youth ages 13 through 24 in 2006.

- African American and Hispanic youth are disproportionately affected by the HIV and AIDS pandemic. Although only 17 percent of the adolescent population in the United States is African American, these teens experienced 69 percent of new AIDS cases among teens in 2006. Latinos ages 20–24 experienced 23 percent of new AIDS cases in 2006 but represented only 18 percent of U.S. young adults.

- A November 2006 study of declining pregnancy rates among teens concluded that the reduction in teen pregnancy between 1995 and 2002 was primarily the result of increased use of contraceptives. However, new data from the Centers for Disease Control and Prevention's National Center for Health Statistics (NCHS) show that teen birth rates are again on the rise.

- The NCHS reports a five percent national increase between 2005 and 2007 in teenage birthrates in the U.S.; from 40.5 to 42.5 births per 1,000 young women aged 15–19.

- Approximately one in five teens reports some kind of abuse in a romantic relationship, with girls who experience dating violence having sex earlier than their peers and being less likely to use birth control and more likely to engage in a wide variety of high-risk behaviors.

Research clearly shows that comprehensive sex education programs do not encourage teens to start having sexual intercourse; do not increase the frequency with which teens have intercourse; and do not increase the number of a teen's sexual partners. At the same time, evaluations of publicly funded abstinence-only programs have repeatedly shown no positive changes in sexual behaviors over time. Young people need honest, effective sex education—not ineffective, shame-based abstinence-only programs.

| "*[Virginity] pledges seem to delay sex for some kids some of the time.*"

Virginity Pledges Prevent Some Teens from Having Sex

Steven Martino

For some teens, virginity pledges delay the start of sexual activity, claims the author of the following viewpoint. That some teens fail to keep their pledge makes sense, as teen attitudes change, he reasons. Thus, virginity pledges are most effective among younger teens and for those teens with solid religious backgrounds, the author maintains. The likelihood of keeping the pledge also increases when taken without pressure from the school or community, he asserts. Since pledges work for some teens, comprehensive sex education programs should include them as an option, he concludes. Steven Martino is a behavioral scientist at the RAND Corporation, a centrist think tank.

As you read, consider the following questions:

1. In Martino's view, what are the benefits of delaying the start of sex?
2. According to the author, on what age group did the RAND study focus?

3. What percentages of boys and girls have sex as teenagers, according to the author?

Over the past decade [beginning around 1999], millions of teens in the United States have made formal pledges to delay sex until they are married. Virginity pledges are part of a wider abstinence movement that has been a controversial approach to sex education.

Essentially, the available research suggests that teaching abstinence alone to teenagers does not work—they are no more likely to delay the start of sexual activity than other teenagers. But research has not been so clear regarding virginity pledges specifically.

Delaying the Start of Sexual Activity

Some studies have found that pledges may help young people delay the start of sexual activity. This would be important regardless of one's religious or moral stance on sexual activity, because we know that delaying the start of sex reduces a teenager's risk of an unintended pregnancy and contracting a sexually transmitted disease.

The latest study on the issue, published in the January [2009] issue of the journal *Pediatrics*, seems to throw cold water on the idea that virginity pledges do much good, finding no difference in sexual activity between pledgers and nonpledgers. Those findings appear to be in direct conflict with those of a similar study I led at the RAND Corporation, published last summer in the *Journal of Adolescent Health*.

So which study is right? The truth is that pledges seem to delay sex for some kids some of the time.

Virginity pledges do not work in the strictest sense of delaying sex until marriage. Almost everyone has sex before they are married (95 percent of Americans), and that includes those who take virginity pledges.

That pledges fail is understandable. Teens' relationship circumstances change. Their perspectives may change. What matters

Pledges May Reduce STD Rates

[A] study found that virginity pledging during adolescence was . . . associated with lower rates of STD [sexually transmitted disease] infection among young adults. The STD rate among pledgers averaged 25 percent lower than the rate of non-pledgers of the same age, gender, race, family background, and religiosity. Significantly, the study found that virginity pledging was a stronger predictor of STD reduction than condom use on five different measures of STDs.

Christine C. Kim and Robert Rector,
"Evidence of the Effectiveness of Abstinence
Education: An Update," Heritage Foundation
Backgrounder, *February 19, 2010.*

is that at the time young people take a virginity pledge, they express a desire to delay sex. Taking a virginity pledge may help them to do so.

So, who are the "some kids" for whom virginity pledges seem to work? They seem to be most (perhaps solely) effective among younger teens. The new *Pediatrics* study investigated the effectiveness of pledges taken at age 16 or older. In contrast, the RAND study focused on pledges taken between the ages of 12 and 17, or earlier.

Pledges also seem to work for only a limited period, or stage of life. The RAND study followed youth for 3 years until they were 15 to 20 years old, and found that 42 percent of pledgers remained virgins, while only 33 percent of similar nonpledgers did so.

The new *Pediatrics* study followed participants for five years after they reported having taken a pledge, until they were 20 or older, and found that they typically had sex for the first time at age 21. By that time, pledgers and nonpledgers appear equally likely to have had sex. If the pledge delays sex until after the teen years, rather than until marriage, there would still be significant health benefits.

Part of a Comprehensive Program

With this knowledge, the most prudent course of action is to offer virginity pledges as part of a comprehensive program of sex education that includes information on birth control methods and condoms.

After all, most young people do not take virginity pledges, and most (65 percent of boys and 70 percent of girls) have sex as teenagers. Even many virginity pledgers will have sex as teenagers, and they need to know how to protect themselves from unintended pregnancy and sexually transmitted diseases when they do.

Should all kids pledge? The answer is clearly "no." The RAND study showed that pledges work for teens with strong religious backgrounds and less positive attitudes toward sex, and who have parents that keep close track of them. Other work indicates pledges must be freely undertaken and that pledges are ineffective if all kids in a school or community take them.

Instead, we should make virginity pledges available for those young people who sincerely wish to make a commitment to abstinence, and provide all young people with the education and skills they need to protect themselves from unintended pregnancy, sexually transmitted diseases, and emotional harm once they do become sexually active.

> "There is something wrong with a law
> that forces a judge to brand a young
> man as a rapist . . . for the rest of his
> life simply for having sex with someone
> before her 16th birthday."

Consensual Sex Among Teens Should Not Be Criminalized

Martha Kempner

Laws that criminalize sex with minors can lead to absurd re-sults when teens engage in consensual sex, maintains the au-thor of the following viewpoint. While society should protect minors from predatory adults, lawmakers did not design age-of-consent laws to make rapists out of teens only a few years older than their intimate partners, she reasons. Nor should laws force these teens to register as sex offenders for the rest of their lives, the author claims. While legal experts debate how to resolve these is-sues, teens must learn to think critically about the consequences of having consensual sex, she concludes. Martha Kempner writes on issues related to sexual and reproductive health and rights.

As you read, consider the following questions:

1. What did Kempner realize about her own sexual experience as a teen when she read about young men who went to jail for having sex with their teen girlfriends?
2. What are the four factors that influence state statutory rape laws, according to the author?
3. What distinctions do laws based solely on age not see, according to Kempner and Dr. Elizabeth Schroeder?

Last month [February 2012], my husband forwarded me [an] article from the *Daily Beast* and I haven't been able to get it out of my mind since. The article focuses on a few young men who went to jail and wound up on sex offender registries ostensibly for having sex with their teenage girlfriends. While the young men were teenagers themselves, at 18 the law considered them adults whereas their girlfriends at 14 and 15 were under the legal age of consent. Now, in fairness, neither of these boys went to jail just for having sex with an underage girl, there were aggravating circumstances—one punched his girlfriend's father and both violated judges' orders to stay away from the girls.

Still, all I could think about was that what started out as a somewhat typical high school relationship (a senior boy with a freshman or sophomore girlfriend is not at all that unusual) essentially ruined these young men's lives. Not only did they spend time in jail and postpone any future plans, their names now sit on sex offender registries alongside those of serial rapist, child pornographers, and pedophiles.

Not Unusual Relationships

And as is human nature, all I could think about was my own life story. Once upon a time, a couple of decades ago or so, I was in one of those not unusual relationships between a sophomore girl and a senior boy. In true high school style, we were fixed up by friends at the beginning of my sophomore year and had an on-again-off-again flirtation throughout the fall and winter (too much of which involved me watching from a distance as his relationship with a perky senior named Suzanne played out in the halls between classes). But by spring they had broken up and one fateful Wednesday he called. From there we began what would be my first serious and my first sexual relationship.

By the time we had sex, we had been together for many months and professed our love for each other, I had nursed him back to puffy-cheeked health after he'd had his wisdom teeth out and he had spent a great deal of time with my family on Cape Cod. Though I can't say it was a perfect relationship or the balance of power was entirely equal (he held some advantage by virtue of being older and more experienced), I can assure you that the sexual aspect of our relationship was consensual, mutually pleasurable, non-exploitative, honest, and protected from pregnancy and STDs [sexually transmitted diseases]. (Years later as a sexuality educator, these are among the litmus tests I would suggest to teens.)

The problem that really didn't occur to me until last week, however, is that from a legal standpoint it was not a consensual relationship. In Massachusetts—which has one of the least nuanced laws regarding age of consent—a person under 16 cannot give consent, and I was three months shy of my 16th birthday that summer. So, though I saw it as a normal and mostly positive sexual experience, had authorities been notified of it for whatever reason, they would have declared it a crime.

This realization had my head swimming with questions. Should we really treat teenagers who have sex with other teenagers as criminals? Should our legal system play any role in regulating "consensual" teen sexual behavior? Is there a way to protect teens from exploitation without making them vulnerable to unnecessary prosecution? And what does all of this say about how society handles teen sex?

Statutory Rape Laws

Statutory rape laws (which are called by a plethora of other names) refer to those laws that "criminalize voluntary sexual acts involving a minor that would be legal if not for the age of one or more of the participants." The premise behind these laws is that until a certain age, young people are incapable of giving their consent for sexual behavior. . . .

Lawmakers seem to have attempted to account for variations in relationships. The laws are certainly more nuanced than I had expected, though above anything else, these laws are complicated. Each state has its own law and decides a number of factors for itself, including age of consent, minimum age of "victim," age differential, and minimum age of "perpetrator" in order to prosecute.

- *Age of consent.* This is the age at which an individual *can* legally consent to sexual intercourse under any circumstances.

- *Minimum age of victim.* This is the age below which an individual *cannot* legally consent to sexual intercourse under any circumstance.

- *Age differential.* If the victim is above the minimum age but below the age of consent, the age differential is the maximum age difference between the victim and the perpetrator where an individual *can* legally consent to sexual intercourse.

- *Minimum of age of defendant in order to prosecute.* This is the age below which an individual *cannot* be prosecuted for engaging in sexual activities with minors.

Anyone else confused by these distinctions?

Only 12 states have a single age of consent below which an individual cannot consent to sexual intercourse and above which they can. As I mentioned earlier, Massachusetts is one of those states—the age of consent there is simply 16. That leaves 39 other states where the laws are more complicated. I found that the only way I could follow them was to look at some specific examples.

(These particular examples were spelled out in a report prepared for the U.S. Department of Health and Human Service in 2003 so there is possibility that some laws have changed since.)

A Varying Focus Among States

In most states, the law takes into account both the age of the victim and the difference in ages between the victim and the perpetrator. In my home state of New Jersey, for example, the age of consent is 16 but "individuals who are at least 13 years of age can legally engage in sexual activities if the defendant is less than 4 years older than the victim." Just so we're clear, this means that the high school sexual experiences I described earlier which were illegal because we were on vacation in Massachusetts would have been just fine if we'd been at home.

In fact, some states focus on the age difference between the two individuals. The District of Columbia, for example, says that it's illegal to engage in sexual intercourse with someone who is under the age of 16 if the perpetrator is four or more years older than the victim. But other states like to make it even more complicated by taking into account the age of both parties. Washington state's laws say that sexual intercourse with someone who is at least 14 but less than 16 is illegal if the defendant is four or more years older but changes the age gap for victims under 14 "in cases where the victim is less than 14 years of age (three years), further decreasing if the victim is less than 12 years of age (two years)." This would mean that in both of these states the case of a 15-year-old girl with an 18-year-old boyfriend would not be illegal.

Other states, however, focus on the age of the perpetrator either on its own or along with the age of the victim. Both Nevada and Ohio, for example, say that perpetrators cannot be prosecuted if they are under 18, thus the two 16-year-olds are safe from prosecution but the 15-year-old's 18-year-old boyfriend is not.

But wait, it gets even more complicated than that because many states make a distinction between sexual contact and sexual intercourse. That's right; there are instances in which activities that under different circumstances we might refer to as foreplay, sexplay, fooling around, or "outercourse" can be illegal depending on the age of the participants. In Connecticut, for example, engaging in *sexual intercourse* with someone who is less than 16 is legal under certain circumstances but *sexual contact* with someone who is less than 15 is illegal regardless of the age of the perpetrator.

So are we supposed to give our teens law books or maybe decoder rings as they head out on a weekend date? Don't we think teens already have enough to worry about when it comes to choosing which sexual behaviors they are going to engage in with a partner?

No Universal Agreement

Obviously, one problem with creating an age of consent law is that there is no universal agreement as to when it is "okay" for teens to have sex. As Dr. Elizabeth Schroeder, the executive director of Answer, a national sexuality education organization that serves young people and the adults who teach them, explains:

> We always tell young people that there's no one right age at which it's okay to start being in a sexual relationship—because with a few exceptions, age is not necessarily the defining factor. We can all agree that, say, 11 or 12 is far too young to be in a sexual relationship, but as we get into the teen years, opinions vary. Readiness has to do with maturity, knowledge about and ability to practice safer sex, whether the decision is in line with that person's values, etc. I've known teens who are more responsible about their sexual relationships than some people in their 30s.

Clearly laws based solely on age do not see these distinctions but it seems like those laws based on age differences aren't getting it either. We've all heard about cases like the ones discussed in the *Daily Beast* article and I'm sure we can all think

A Sex Offender for Life

Human Rights Watch spoke with or came across the stories of a number of men and women who because of consensual teenage sex with willing partners must now register as sex offenders—in some cases for life—and suffer all the adverse consequences that come with that status. For example, in Georgia, a 26-year-old married woman was made to register as a sex offender for life and had to move from her home because it falls within an area in which sex offenders are prohibited from living, because as a teenager she had oral sex with a willing fellow high school student when she was 17 and he was 15. It is difficult, if not impossible, to fathom what public safety purpose is served by subjecting her to registration, community notification, and residency restriction laws.

Human Rights Watch, No Easy Answers:
Sex Offender Laws in the United States, *2007.*

of other nightmare scenarios; the mother who turns her daughter's slightly older boyfriend in because she doesn't like him, the young woman upset about being dumped who turns in her older boyfriend, or the guidance counselor who feels compelled to pass rumors on to authorities. Many of the sexual experts I spoke with also expressed concern for gay and lesbian young people whom they felt were even more vulnerable to irate parents who want to "throw the book" at an older partner who they blame for "turning their kid gay."

Expert Outrage over Laws

The experts were all distressed about the possibility of such cases and outrage over how these laws were being applied was a common refrain. J. Dennis Fortenberry, a professor of pediatrics at

Indiana University who researches adolescent sexual behavior, said: "This enthusiastic jailing under the guise of protection is in fact an abuse of power and sexual rights." Pepper Schwartz, an author and sociologist at the University of Washington, referred to these laws as "a very blunt dangerous instrument for a very complex culturally variable circumstance." She pointed out that such laws would cause any mother of a son to fear "that your child could do something unwise but not aggressive or without invitation that would ruin his life forever."

Many of the educators I spoke with pointed out just how normal and common sexual behavior among teens under the age of consent is. One study found that 23 percent of 15-year-olds [and] 34 percent of 16-year-olds have had vaginal intercourse. According to the CDC's [Centers for Disease Control and Prevention] Youth Risk Behavior Surveillance [System], nearly two-thirds of high school students have had sex before they graduate. Clearly we shouldn't be sending them all to jail instead of college. Fortenberry notes that given the average age of first sex is between 16 and 17, "the number of people you would have to prosecute if the law was uniformly and equally applied would be staggering."

Unequally Enforced

And that is one of his main complaints with age of consent laws—they are not equally enforced or enforceable. Teens are in many ways at the mercy of an enraged parent or an over-eager law enforcement official. As one expert pointed out, "all you need is one police officer at lover's lane." Another expert I spoke with told me a story of a case she had learned about many years ago involving a girl who was not quite 13 and a 17-year-old boy who had sex one time. The incident was brought to the attention of a guidance counselor who reported it to the authorities because she was under 14. Everyone involved in the case—both teens and both sets of parents—agreed that the sex was consensual and that if anything the girl was the aggressor in the incident. While they were able to prevent the teenage boy from going to prison, despite this agreement, they were not able to keep his name off the state's sex offender registry.

It is these registries that have experts most alarmed and upset because they have lifetime implications. States began to create such registries in the 1990s with the intention of protecting community members from violent sex offenders who were at a high risk of reoffending. The Reverend Debra Haffner, executive director of the Religious Institute notes:

> These laws were never intended to place teenagers on offender registries for the rest of their lives. What we're seeing here is the confluence of two panics—that of teens having sex coupled with the panic about offenders.

She added that age of consent and registry laws, "Equate all kinds of legal violations so that this teenager is listed with people who are serial rapists of children." . . .

What's the Alternative?

Amid all the outrage over these laws, the experts with whom I spoke all understood that we do have an obligation to protect young people from exploitation. Haffner likened this to the need for sexual harassment laws in the workplace: "We do have an interest in making it clear that there are laws to protect people when they don't have power."

Creating fair laws to do this, of course, remains a challenge.

One place to start, however, would be to change the classification of statutory rape laws in order to make a distinction between the teen lover whose partner was legally too young and the serial rapist or child molester. As Schwartz put it:

> These laws started out with a good intention—to stop seduction of children by adults—but the teenage years are a very different proposition. Even if we want to make it a crime for someone to have sex with a person more than three or four

years younger or with a person under 13, sex offense isn't the crime. You're not a sex offender.

Or we might want to do away with our rush to punish teen sex and instead work to come to a better understanding—both as individuals and a society—of what consent really is. As educators, everyone I spoke to, wished for a national dialogue on these issues and for programs that would help teens handle consent issues. Fortenberry's wish list included giving teens:

> Good refusal skills as well as relationship literacy that helps them understand what a good relationship is and how to judge when they feel truly ready to have sex.

Getting Teens to Think Critically

In my mind, pretty much all issues around teen sexual behavior come down to critical thinking. We want teens to be able look critically at a situation and assess whether it's a good idea to engage in any given sexual behavior. In *Talk About Sex*, a resource aimed directly at teens that we created while I was at SIECUS [Sexuality Information and Education Council of the United States], Monica Rodriguez and I asked teenagers to look at a number of factors when deciding what they wanted to do in a sexual relationship. We suggested they take into account the relationship (old friend, new acquaintance), the specific situation (upstairs at a party, in a parked car), and their motivations (to feel closer to a person, to gain popularity, to keep a partner from breaking up with them). We also suggested that they ask themselves if they had the other person's consent, if everyone was being honest, if they felt safe, if they felt exploited, and if they were protecting themselves and their partner from pregnancy and STDs.

I believe that given the skills to think critically about all of these aspects of sexual relationships many young people would themselves weed out the relationships that we as adults are most concerned about—whether it's a 15-year-old girl admitting that having sex with her 19-year-old boyfriend was really an attempt to prove she was mature enough to be with him or a 20-year-old boy questioning the wisdom of dating someone who is still in high school. But it is our responsibility as adults to teach them how to assess these situations.

It is also our responsibility as adults to think critically ourselves about the benefits and risks of the laws we make and we how we apply them. No matter how good the intent behind it, there is something wrong with a law that forces a judge to brand a young man as a rapist thereby severely limiting his opportunities for housing and employment for the rest of his life simply for having sex with someone before her 16th birthday. And it is our responsibility as adults to fix it.

Periodical and Internet Sources Bibliography

The following articles have been chosen to supplement the diverse views presented in this chapter.

Nicholas Bakalar	"Teenagers Having Sex Are a Minority," *New York Times*, November 14, 2011.
Michael Darflinger	"Honesty Is the Best Policy: Sex Education and Accuracy," *Journal of Legal Medicine*, 2008.
Economist	"Unjust and Ineffective: America Has Pioneered the Harsh Punishment of Sex Offenders. Does it Work?" August 6, 2009.
N. Joycelyn Elders	"A Collision of Culture and Nature: How Our Fear of Teen Sexuality Leaves Teens More Vulnerable," *RH Reality Check*, July 19, 2011.
Guttmacher Institute	"Facts on American Teens' Sexual and Reproductive Health," February 2012. www.guttmacher.org.
Kierra Johnson	"The Myth of the Teen Pregnancy Epidemic," *Huffington Post*, July 21, 2010.
Christine C. Kim and Robert Rector	"Evidence on the Effectiveness of Abstinence Education: An Update," *Backgrounder* (Heritage Foundation), February 19, 2010.
Joan Malin	"Sex Education: Don't Fear It, Use It," *New York Times*, November 8, 2011.
Emily Mills	"Kids Need to Know About Sex," *Isthmus*, December 2011.
Barbara Miner	"We're Here. We're Sexual. Get Used to It," *Colorlines*, May–June 2008.
Abigail Pesta	"Should Teens Be Jailed for Sex Offenses?" *Daily Beast*, January 25, 2012.
Jennie Yabroff	"The Myths of Teen Sex," *Newsweek*, June 9, 2008.

CHAPTER 3

What Impact Do Media and Technology Have on Teen Dating?

Chapter Preface

One of the more hotly contested issues in the teen dating debate is the impact of technology. The number of teens with access to digital communication technology has been steadily rising, according to surveys by Cox Communications and the National Center for Missing and Exploited Children (NCMEC). At their 5th Annual National Teen Summit on Internet Safety in 2010, Cox and NCMEC revealed that 84 percent of surveyed teens had a cell phone and the same percentage also had a social network profile. While 82 percent claimed to be aware that online posts can affect their reputations, only 32 percent thought information they posted online would have a negative impact on their future. According to John Walsh, child advocate and host of the Summit, "It's the age-old problem of kids thinking they are invulnerable."[1] He adds, "It's not that they don't understand there can be consequences; it's that they believe it cannot happen to them."[2] Peter Picard, who represents the company that conducted the survey, agrees. "Full of the confidence of youth and still under the protective umbrella of parents, teens simply feel immune to danger and consequence."[3] Although posting embarrassing or reputation-altering information online is indeed a threat, digital communication can pose other serious problems for dating teens.

Text messaging, for example, can be used by an abusive partner to stalk, harass, and threaten. Author Jill Murray, an expert on dating violence, claims that "textual harassment" is "part and parcel of everyday abusive dating relationship[s] now."[4] Victims can receive insults or demands any time of day and night. As many as one hundred or more texts can arrive each day while teens are in class, at home, or at the movies. According to *Washington Post* staff writer Donna St. George, textual harassment "can be insidious, because messages pop up at the sender's will: "Where r u? Who r u with? Why didn't u answer me?"[5] When relationships end, these messages can increase in number and become more threatening. Demi Brae, the daughter of Gary Cuccia, now a teen dating violence education advocate, was murdered a day after her sixteenth birthday in 2007. After she broke up with her boyfriend, he texted her repeatedly. He claimed that she could not live without him and begged her over and over to allow him to see her. When she relented, he came to her home when she was alone and stabbed her 16 times in her own living room. The family was unaware of the texting, which Cuccia claims is part of the problem. "When I was growing up, we had one phone in the whole house, and if you were fighting with your girlfriend, everybody knew about it,"[6] he claims. Not only is texting private, but because texting is also perceived by many teens as a normal part of life, some do not see excessive texting as a sign of abuse. Thus, activists claim, parents should pay more attention to their children's texting.

Parents can, in fact, find many applications to monitor their children digitally. A 2011 Pew Research Center survey found that two-thirds of parents did indeed check their children's digital footprints. For example, one grandmother, Mary Cofield, offered her 15-year-old granddaughter a smartphone with full privileges, as long as the grandmother was allowed to monitor her use. Cofield uses a program called uKnowKids.com, which searches her granddaughter's social networking pages and text messages, alerting her to potentially inappropriate communication. The software also translates the language teens speak in the digital world. However, Cofield says that she does not interfere with boy trouble or conflicts with friends. "If I did that, she would definitely go underground,"[7] Cofield claims.

Some parents are not as concerned about the impact of technology on teens. CBSNews.com editorial director Dick Meyer admits that "teenagers seem to have harnessed technology to communicate more and better, even if it seem[s] like less and worse to me and my fellow fossils."[8] Nevertheless, Meyer fears that technology does put teenagers at risk for what he calls increased exposure: "more exposure to everything, good and bad: peer pressure, marketing, sin, vice, opportunity, good works, other lands and people. Something like that is too big to be labeled good or bad. It is too big for teenagers not to jump into and too big for grown-ups not to worry about. We're all doing our jobs."[9]

Clearly, whether technology has a positive or negative impact on teens and dating relationships continues to be controversial. The authors in the following chapter express their views in answer to this question. Whether teen use of technology requires parental monitoring or broader intervention remains to be seen. Indeed, Dick Meyer reasons, "I do think the pace of change in daily life caused by technology in this period is great by historical measure. The Internet is a big invention. It is hard to measure such things in the present tense."[10]

Notes

1. Quoted in National Center for Missing and Exploited Children, "Cox Survey Shows 46 Percent of Teens Allow Unrestricted Access to Their Online Profiles and 62 Percent Don't Check with Parents Before Posting Photos," June 15, 2011. www.missingkids .com.
2. National Center, "Cox Survey."
3. National Center, "Cox Survey."
4. Quoted in Donna St. George, "Text Messages Become a Growing Weapon in Dating Violence," Washington Post, June 21, 2010.
5. St. George, "Text Messages."
6. St. George, "Text Messages."
7. Quoted in Somini Sengupta, "'Big Brother'? No, It's Parents," New York Times, June 25, 2012.
8. Dick Meyer, "Teens, Tech, and the Tides of History," CBS News, February 11, 2009. www.cbsnews.com.
9. Meyer, "Teens, Tech."
10. Meyer, "Teens, Tech."

"*Press coverage and policy discussions have focused on how teens are using or misusing cell phones as part of their sexual interactions and explorations.*"

Sexting Can Be a Serious Problem for Dating Teens

Amanda Lenhart

Teens who are sexting and sending sexually suggestive, nude or nearly nude cell phone images of themselves face social and legal consequences, claims the author of the following viewpoint. Some states prosecute sexting teens for producing and distributing child pornography, she asserts. Although teens generally sext as part of or in hopes of establishing a romantic relationship, recipients often forward these images to others, the author maintains. Because sexting is less common among teens whose parents limit texting, concerned parents should consider setting limits, she concludes. Amanda Lenhart directs research on teens, children, and families at the Pew Research Center's Internet and American Life Project.

As you read, consider the following questions:

1. According to Lenhart, how has the use of cell phones changed since Pew's 2004 survey of teens?

Amanda Lenhart, "Teens and Sexting," Pew Internet and American Life Project, December 15, 2009, pp. 2–10. Copyright © 2009 by the Pew Internet and American Life Project. All rights reserved. Reproduced by permission.

2. How are some state legislatures responding to the prosecution of sexting teens, in the author's view?

3. According to the author, are teens more or less likely to sext if their parents view the contents of their phones?

Since the Pew Research Center's Internet and American Life Project first started tracking teen cell phone use, the age at which American teens acquire their first cell phone has consistently grown younger. In Pew Internet's 2004 survey of teens, 18% of teens age 12 owned a cell phone. In 2009, 58% of 12-year-olds own a cell phone. We also have found that cell phone ownership increases dramatically with age: 83% of teens age 17 now own a cell phone, up from 64% in 2004.

At the same time the level of adoption has been growing, the capacity of these cell phones has also changed dramatically. Many teens now use their phones not just for calling, but also to access the internet and to take and share photos and videos. In our survey of 800 youth ages 12–17 conducted from June 26 to September 24 [2009], we found that 75% of all teens those ages own a cell phone and 66% of teens use text messaging.

Increasing Concerns About Sexting

Texting has become a centerpiece in teen social life, and parents, educators and advocates have grown increasingly concerned about the role of cell phones in the sexual lives of teens and young adults. In particular, over the past year [2009], press coverage and policy discussions have focused on how teens are using or misusing cell phones as part of their sexual interactions and explorations. The greatest amount of concern has focused on "sexting" or the creating, sharing and forwarding of sexually suggestive nude or nearly nude images by minor teens.

Both laws and law enforcement practices around sexting are emerging to deal with the issue and they vary significantly from jurisdiction to jurisdiction. Some law enforcement officers and district attorneys have begun prosecuting teens who created and shared such images under laws generally reserved for producers and distributors of child pornography.

Conflict over Enforcement

An incident in Pennsylvania that unfolded earlier this year highlighted the conflict between those committed to strictly enforcing the law and those who believe that such enforcement is a heavy-handed response to social problem best handled outside of the legal system in a way that treats minors as a special case (as in other parts of the justice system). In Pennsylvania, a local district attorney [DA] threatened to charge 17 students who were either pictured in images or found with "provocative" images on their cell phones with prosecution under child pornography laws unless they agreed to participate in a five-week after school program and probation. The parents of two of the girls countersued the DA with the assistance of the American Civil Liberties Union, who argued that the images did not constitute pornography and that the girls could not be charged as they did not consent to the distribution of the images that pictured them. Similar incidents occurred in Massachusetts, Ohio, and several other states. One notable incident in Florida left 18-year-old Philip Alpert listed as registered sex offender for the next 25 years after he was convicted of sending nude images of his 16-year-old girlfriend to family and friends after an argument. Teens are being charged with everything from "disorderly conduct" and "illegal use of a minor in nudity-oriented material" to felony "sexual abuse of children . . . , criminal [use] of a communications facility, or open lewdness."

Legislatures in a handful of states are stepping in to consider making laws that downgrade the charges for creating or trading sexually suggestive images of minors by text from felonies to misdemeanors. In 2009, the Vermont and Utah state legislatures downgraded the penalties for minors and first-time perpetrators of "sexting." Ohio has legislation pending to criminalize, at a milder level, sexting between minors.

In December 2008, the National Campaign to Prevent Teen and Unplanned Pregnancy and their research partners released a study called "Sex and Tech" that examined the role of technology in the sex lives of teens and young adults. In addition to the National Campaign's online survey, Cox Communications, partnered with National Center for Missing and Exploited Children and Harris Interactive, and MTV in partnership with the Associated Press [AP] have also released findings from online surveys on the topic. In the National Campaign study, 19% of teens ages 13–19 who participated in the survey said they had sent a sexually suggestive picture or video of themselves to someone via email, cell phone or by another mode, and 31% had received a nude or semi-nude picture from someone else. In the Cox study done in March 2009, 9% of teens ages 13–18 had sent a sexually suggestive text message or email with nude or nearly-nude photos, 3% had forwarded one, and 17% had received a sexually suggestive text message or email with nude or nearly nude photos. The MTV-AP poll conducted in September reports that 1 in 10 young adults between the ages of 14 and 24 have shared a naked image of themselves with someone else and 15% have had someone send them naked pictures or videos of themselves. Another 8% of young adults have had someone send them naked images of someone else they know personally.

Studying Teen Sexting

In our nationally-representative telephone survey conducted from June to September we asked teens whether they had sent or received sexually suggestive nude or nearly nude photos or videos of themselves or of someone they knew on their cell phones. Partnering with the University of Michigan, in October we conducted a series of focus groups with teens ages 12–18 and during those groups, teens took a private paper survey in which they wrote about their experiences with sexting.

These questions focus on the sending and receiving of images via cell phone, and do not address suggestive text messages without visual content or those shared by other means (such as email or online social networks). We chose this strategy because the policy community and advocates are primarily concerned with the legality of sharing images and because the mobile phone is increasingly the locus of teens' personal, and seemingly private, communication.

The Pew Internet survey data show that 4% of all cell-owning teens ages 12–17 report sending a sexually suggestive nude or nearly-nude photo or video of themselves to someone else. The data reveal no difference in this practice related to gender: Girls and boys are equally as likely to have sent a suggestive picture to another person. The oldest teens in our sample—those aged 17—are the most likely to report having sent a sexually suggestive image via text with 8% of 17-year-olds having sent one, compared to 4% of those age 12. But otherwise, there is little variation across age groups in the likelihood of having sent a sexual image by text. Teens who paid for all of the costs associated with their cell phone were more likely to report sending sexual images of themselves by text, with 17% of these teens sending sexually suggestive texts compared to just 3% of teens who did not pay for or only paid for a portion of the cost of their cell phone. Overall, 70% of teens have a cell phone that someone else, usually a parent, pays for, 19% pay part of the costs and 10% pay all of the costs of their cell phone.

When it comes to receiving images, 15% of those ages 12–17 have received a sexually suggestive nude or nearly nude photo or video of someone they know on their cell phone. Older teens ages 14–17 are more likely than younger teens to report receiving such images or videos: 18% of older teens have received an image versus 6% of teens ages 12–13 who have received such content. The data show a steady increase in likelihood of receipt of sexually suggestive images via text by age, with just 4% of 12-year-olds receiving these images or videos compared to 20% of 16-year-olds and 30% of 17-year-olds. There are no statistically significant differences in reports of receipt of these images by gender.

There are some indications that teens who send and receive suggestive images via text message are likely to be those whose

Teens Are Unaware of the Implications of Sexting

Seventy-three percent of teenagers say they know sexting can have negative consequences, but they do it anyway. Why? According to psychologist Susan Lipkins, a national authority on teens and young adults, sixty-six percent of the girls who sent sexts did it to be flirtatious. Fifty-two percent of girls send sexts as a sexy present for a guy and forty percent of the girls said the sexts were sent as a joke. Clearly teens do not understand the serious social and legal implications of sexting.

Linda L. Barkacs and Craig B. Barkacs,
"Do You Think I'm Sexty? Minors and Sexting:
Teenage Fad or Child Pornography?," Journal
of Legal, Ethical and Regulatory Issues,
vol. 13, no. 2, 2010.

phones are more central to their lives than less intense cell phone users. For instance, teens who send any type of text message are more likely than teens who do not text to say they have received a sexually suggestive image on their cell phone, with 16% of texters receiving these images compared to 7% of teens who do not use text messaging. Teens with unlimited text messaging plans—75% of teens with cell phones—are also more likely to report receiving sexually suggestive texts with 18% of teens with unlimited plans receiving nude or nearly nude images or video via their phones, compared to 8% of those with limited plans and 4% of those who pay per message.

Teens who receive sexually suggestive images on their cell phones are more likely to say that they use the phone to entertain themselves when bored; 80% of sexting recipients say they use their phones to combat boredom, while 67% of teens who have not received suggestive images on their phone say the same. Teens who have received these images are also less likely to say that they turn off their phones when it is not otherwise required—68% of receiving teens say they generally do not turn off their phones when they do not have to, and 46% of teens who have not received suggestive images by text report the same "always on" behavior.

Three Basic Sexting Scenarios

Teens in our focus groups outlined three general scenarios in which sexually suggestive images are shared or forwarded. In one situation, images are shared between two romantic partners, in lieu of, as a prelude to, or as a part of sexual activity.

"[I've sexted] a few times," wrote one 9th/10th grade boy. "Just between my girlfriend and I. Just my girlfriend sending pictures of herself to me and me sending pictures of myself to her."

"Yeah, I've sent them to my boyfriend," said a 9th/10th grade girl. "Everybody does it."

An 11th/12th grade girl talked about sexting as part of an experimental phase for teens who are not yet sexually active.

"I think it was more common in middle school, because kids are afraid to do face-to-face contact sexually. In high school, kids don't need the pictures. They'll just hang out with that person romantically."

For other teens, sexting is one part of a sexual relationship.

"Yes, I do. I only do it with my girlfriend b/c we have already been sexually active with each other," wrote one older high school age boy. "It's not really a big deal."

Forwarding Images

However, these images sent between romantic partners can easily be forwarded (with or without the subject's knowledge) to friends or classmates and beyond.

"This girl sent pictures to her boyfriend," wrote one older high school boy. "Then they broke up and he sent them to his friend, who sent them to like everyone in my school. Then she was supposed to come to my school because she got kicked out of her school because it was a Catholic school . . . it ruined high school for her."

A middle school boy wrote, "Yeah, [I get sexts] once a year, [from] people who have girlfriends . . . usually the sender had it sent from his girlfriend and sent it to everyone . . . it's no big deal and it doesn't happen very often."

Another high school girl explained, "I've heard of people getting these types of pictures and usually its someone's girlfriend but the people that receive them aren't even the person that they are dating—they are sent to like ten other guys, for example, like the guy's friends with something saying 'I can't believe she did this.'"

Another younger high school-aged girl wrote, "Yeah, it happens a lot, my friends do it all the time, it's not a big deal. Sometimes people will get into fights with their exs, and so they will send the nudes as blackmail, but it's usually when or after you've been dating someone."

Hoping for Romance

But other images are sent between friends, or between two people where at least one of the pair is hoping to become romantically involved.

"If a guy wants to hookup with you, he'll send a picture of his private parts or a naked picture of him[self]. It happens about 10 times a month," explained one older high school girl. "It's mostly the guys I date or just a guy that . . . really wants to hook up with you. I'm not really that type of person [who sends sexts], but I have friends who have."

"Almost all the time it's a single girl sending to a single guy," wrote a younger high school boy. "Sometimes people trade pictures like 'hey you send me a pic I'll send you one.'"

Another younger high school boy wrote, "Yes I have received some pics that include nudity. Girls will send them sometimes, not often. I don't know why they think it's a good idea but I'm not going to stop it. Sometimes a guy will get one and forward it to all his friends."

One middle school boy wrote, "I have not received or sent, but have asked. It's mostly people I know—I've only asked once."

And another middle school boy wrote, "Well one time this crazy girl who had liked me sent me a nude picture of her for no reason. This was the only time. It was someone I knew for a while but we began to not be friends. [Sending the images was] over the line because they were graphic and completely uncalled for."

Relationship Currency

Sexually suggestive images sent to the privacy of the phone have become a form of relationship currency.

One senior girl reflected: "When I was about 14–15 years old, I received/sent these types of pictures. Boys usually ask for them or start that type of conversation. My boyfriend, or someone I really liked asked for them. And I felt like if I didn't do it, they wouldn't continue to talk to me. At the time, it was no big deal. But now looking back it was definitely inappropriate and over the line."

Another older high school girl wrote about the pressure on girls to share such images: "I haven't, but most of the girls who have are usually pressured by a guy that they like or want to like them, or their boyfriends. It's probably more common than what it seems because most people who get involved in this were probably pressured by someone to do it."

It is important to note that many teens have not sent or received or had sexually suggestive images forwarded to them.

"Um, no . . . things like that [are] never sent to my phone. And no, I've never done it," wrote one middle school girl.

Another older high school girl wrote, "No, I haven't ever sent or received a picture or video on my phone that involves nudity."

A younger high school boy explained his take on sexting: "I don't do that and I don't ask girls—[it's] not right and they wont like [you] as much—they will think of you as a pervert. So I don't."

Attitudes Toward Sexting

In the focus groups, we found that teens' attitudes towards sexting vary widely, from those who do not think it is a major issue to others who think it is inappropriate, "slutty," potentially damaging or illegal. On one end of the spectrum are the teens who view sexting as a safer alternative to real life sexual activity.

"No, [it's not a big deal] we are not having sex, we are sexting," wrote one 9th/10th grade boy. "It's not against my religion or anything."

Another younger high school boy added: "Most people are too shy to have sex. Sexting is not as bad."

Another high school boy wrote "I know people think [sexting] is dangerous, but to me, it's no big deal because I get them a lot."

Other teens avoid it because of their concerns about legality and the potential for public release of the images.

"I have never sent or received a picture involving nudity because I do know that it is illegal," wrote an older high school girl. She continued, "Also, I think texting [sexually suggestive images] is too risky—a friend could take your phone and see it. That's not something you want to be in public. And at my school you can get in trouble for it."

Some teens brand these images, particularly images of girls, as inappropriate and make judgments about the people who appear in them. One older high school boy wrote, "This is common only for girls with 'slut' reputations. They do it to attract attention."

A middle school girl had a similar concern: "I've been asked to send naked pics, but I think that's stupid. You can ruin your reputation. Sometimes I wonder how girls can send naked pics to a boy. I think it's gross. They're disrespecting themselves."

Teens make fine distinctions in what is acceptable and what is unacceptable in transmitted images.

"I like classy girls so I don't like [sexts] as much any more—it makes them look slutty," wrote one younger high school boy. "But [it's] not a big deal if [it's] just a topless photo, but when it's the bottom also it's a lot more serious."

Another middle school girl had a different view of the distinction between "slutty" and nude images. When asked if she had sent sexually suggestive nude or nearly nude images of herself to someone else's cell phone she wrote, "NEVER have and never will. I think I've only sent slutty pics but not naked."

When teens in the focus groups were asked how common they believed sexting to be, the answers covered the spectrum, from infrequent to very common.

"Sexting's not common, but it does happen because girls want everyone to know they 'look good,'" wrote one teen.

"I think it's not very common, but people do it."

"[Sexting's] not common at my school, but I do know a handful of *couples* that do this." [Emphasis hers]

Still, some teens believe sexting is quite prevalent. A high school girl wrote: "I think it's fairly common in my school for people to do this. They see it as a way of flirting that may possibly lead to more for them."

One high school boy wrote that sexting happens a lot "because if someone is going out wit[h] a hot girl and she sends him a message with a picture, then everyone wants to see it."

A younger high school girl wrote, "Yes, [sexting is pretty common] cuz some of my friends do it. [But it's] no big deal I would let my mom see if she wanted."

Another girl in the same focus group wrote, "yeah, it happens a lot, my friends do it all the time, but its not a big deal."

The Parents' Role

What is the role of parents here? One younger high school boy told us that he never sends or receives sexually suggestive images via text because "my mom goes through my phone." However, another high school boy described how he password protected images to keep others from viewing them. He told us that he "get(s) text picture messages from girls because they like me. The picture would have nudity, but I put those on security for my phone." On the Pew Internet telephone survey, teens whose parents said they looked at the contents of their child's cell phone were no more or less likely to send or receive nude or nearly nude images on their phones.

One parental intervention that may relate to a lower likelihood of sending of sexually suggestive images was parental restriction of text messaging. Teens who sent sexually suggestive nude or nearly nude images were less likely to have parents who reported limiting the number of texts or other messages the teen could send. Just 9% of teens who sent sexy images by text had parents who restricted the number of texts or other messages they could send; 28% of teens who didn't send these texts had parents who limited their child's texting.

"While sexting does seem to occur among
a notable minority of adolescents, there
is little reliable evidence that the problem
is as far-reaching as many media reports
have suggested."

The Problem of Teen Sexting
Is Less Common than
First Reported

*Kaitlin Lounsbury, Kimberly J. Mitchell, and
David Finkelhor*

*Public concern over teen sexting—the sending of sexually sugges-
tive images of nude or seminude individuals via cell phone—has
led researchers to varying conclusions, maintain the authors of the
following viewpoint. A review of these studies reveals that while
sexting is a problem for a small group of teens, the problem is not
prevalent, the authors argue. In fact, they claim, many studies have
limitations that reduce their reliability: the definitions of sexting in
some studies are too broad and the age groups studied sometimes
included adults. Kimberly J. Mitchell and David Finkelhor conduct research at the University of New Hampshire's Crimes Against
Children Research Center. Kaitlin Lounsbury graduated with a degree in psychology from the university in May 2012.*

As you read, consider the following questions:

1. According to Lounsbury, Mitchell, and Finkelhor, why was the inclusion of 18- and 19-year-olds in the Sex and Tech Survey a problem?
2. Why does the "one in five" statistic often cited to summarize the Teen Online and Wireless Safety Survey distort the study's true findings, in the authors' opinion?
3. Why do the authors believe that a standardized definition of sexting is needed?

The problem of teen "sexting" has captured a great deal of media attention, causing concern among parents, educators, and law enforcement officials. In reaction to these concerns, a number of studies have been conducted by researchers from many different organizations to estimate the prevalence of the problem, with widely-varying findings. This [viewpoint] will provide an overview of the most widely-cited studies, along with their strengths and weaknesses.

What Is Sexting?

Depending on the study, the term "sexting" has been used to describe a wide variety of activities. It is most commonly used to describe the creation and transmission of sexual images by minors. The majority of attention has been directed toward sexting via cell phone, but the term can apply to any digital media, such as e-mail, instant messaging, and social networking sites. The term can be used for producing and sending images of oneself, receiving images directly from the producer, or forwarding received images to other people.

A core concern about sexting, and what this fact sheet will focus on, is the prevalence of incidents where youth are creating images of themselves or other minors that meet criminal definitions of child pornography. Under current federal laws, any sexually explicit images of minors under age 18 are considered child pornography, *even if the minors created the images themselves.* Some officials have arrested and prosecuted teen "sexters" under child pornography production, possession, and distribution laws.

The following studies were all conducted from 2008 to 2009 and concern the issue of sexting, either as the main focus or as part of a larger study. . . .

The Sex and Tech Survey

One of the first and most commonly cited studies on sexting was conducted by the National Campaign to Prevent Teen and Unplanned Pregnancy with the help of Cosmogirl.com. The survey was conducted using an online sample of 1,280 respondents (653 teens age 13–19 and 627 young adults age 20–26).

Major Findings: 20% of teens, ages 13 to 19, including 18% of teen boys and 22% of teen girls had sent or posted nude or semi-nude pictures or videos of themselves on the Internet or through a cell phone. The majority of teens said they sent sexually suggestive content to boyfriends or girlfriends. However, 21% of teen girls and 39% of teen boys said they sent the content to someone they wanted to date or "hook up" with. Fifteen percent of teens who had sent sexually suggestive content did so to someone they only knew online.

Limitations: There are several points to keep in mind when interpreting the findings of the Sex and Tech Survey. First, the "teens" described in the study included 18- and 19-year-olds. It is legal for these adults to produce and share sexual photos of themselves. However, it is still the "20% of all teens" statistic that is most commonly cited, even though the major concern should be about sexual pictures of minors only, images that could be illegal.

Second, the participants did not constitute a representative sample, meaning that the survey results cannot be considered characteristic of the youth population in general. The teens and young adults participating in the survey had all volunteered to do multiple online surveys through a survey center called TRU. Participants were weighted to reflect the demographic composition of the U.S. population, but the researchers admitted that the respondents did not constitute a probability sample. A recent report from the American Association for Public Opinion Research (AAPOR) advised against using these types of non-probability online panels to estimate the national prevalence of a particular phenomenon.

Finally, the definition of sexting used by these researchers ("nude or semi-nude pictures or video") could include many types of images that are not illegal under federal law. For example, "semi-nude" could include images of youth in bathing suits or underwear, which would generally not be illegal. Since the major concern is the exchange of illegal images of youth, the findings of this study do not accurately address the primary issue at hand.

The Teen Online and Wireless Safety Survey

Less than one year after the Sex and Tech Survey, Cox Communications commissioned Harris Interactive to conduct a similar study looking at teens' online and wireless safety practices. The study was conducted online and the sample included 655 teens ages 13–18 recruited online and weighted to be representative of the U.S. population of teens in that age range.

Major Findings: About one in five teens (19%) had engaged in sexting (sending, receiving, or forwarding text messages or emails with nude or nearly-nude photos) and over one-third knew of a friend who had sent or received these kinds of messages. However, only 12% of teen girls and 6% of teen boys had *sent* a "sext." Sext senders were more likely to be girls (65% vs. 35% boys) and older teens ages 16 to 18 (61% vs. 39% ages 13–15). Nearly all sext senders had also received a sext, although there were many who only received the content. Only 3% of all teens in the study forwarded a sext after receiving it from someone else. Teens mainly sent the messages to boyfriends and girlfriends or someone they had a "crush" on. However, about 1 in 10 sexters said they sent these messages to people they did not know and 18% of sext receivers did not know the person who sent the messages to them.

Limitations: The statement most commonly used to summarize the findings ("one in five teens has engaged in sexting") distorts the true findings of this study. This "one in five" statistic is largely made up of teens who only received the images; only 9% actually produced and sent the messages themselves and only 3% forwarded messages. Production and distribution of sexual images are the primary concern with sexting, because these are the activities that have the highest potential to result in legal ramifications.

There are also problems with the study sample. Like the Sex and Tech Study, 18-year-olds were included in the sample, possibly distorting the findings, because sexting among these individuals would not be illegal. Cox Communications researchers did point out that 8 in 10 of the teens in their sample were under age 18, but the results were not broken down by age. Also, the sample was drawn from an online panel, which experts have advised against using for national prevalence estimates, as previously mentioned.

The AP-MTV Digital Abuse Study

Also in 2009, MTV and the Associated Press [AP] conducted a study on the prevalence of digital abuse, which included questions about sexting. A total of 1,247 respondents age 14 to 24 were surveyed from KnowledgePanel, an online panel that recruits participants using telephone- and mail-based sampling techniques. This recruitment method may have made the sample more representative of the U.S. population than studies that only surveyed online volunteers.

Major Findings: One of the most commonly cited statistics from this report is the finding that almost half of sexually active young people were involved in sexting, which has been described in media reports as "sending nude photos of themselves or their sexual partners via cell phone." Sexting rates were higher among 18- to 24-year-olds (33%) compared to 14- to 17-year-olds (24%).

It was more common for young people (29%) to have *received* messages with "sexual words or images" by cell phone or on the Internet. However, 17% of sext recipients admitted to forwarding the images to someone else, over half of whom shared the images with more than one person, demonstrating that there can be many unintended viewers of these images. Only 1 in 10 had actually shared a naked image of themselves and these rates were higher among females than among males. While females were more likely to *produce* the images (13% vs. 9% of males), males were more likely to *receive* the images (14% vs. 9% of females).

Limitations: Many media reports have misrepresented the actual findings of this study. The findings do indicate that 45% of young people who reported having had sex in the past seven days also reported "at least one sexting related activity," but this includes young people who have only received the images and nowhere does it state that those photos were necessarily of the respondents' sexual partners. The actual percentage of sexually active young people who had shared naked photos of themselves was 17%, compared to 8% of non-sexually active young people. Also, these findings were not broken down by age, so it is possible that they are more applicable to the young adults in the study than to the teenagers.

The South West Grid for Learning and University of Plymouth Sexting Survey

In November 2009, researchers at the South West Grid for Learning in collaboration with the University of Plymouth announced the results to date of an ongoing study on sexting. The head researcher, Dr. Andy Phippen, presented his study as evidence of a "significantly larger problem than we first imagined" and later went on to say that "it is immediately apparent that such practices are cause for concern."

Major Findings: The researchers found that 40% of students knew friends who had sexted, defined as "sharing explicit images electronically." Twenty-seven percent of the students said that sexting happens regularly or "all of the time."

Limitations: A review of the research report suggests that this study should not be included in any estimates of sexting prevalence due to a number of serious flaws. First, the term "sexting" is loosely defined, as previously mentioned, as "the sharing of explicit images electronically." There was little consensus amongst the students over what "explicit" meant, with some stating that topless and nude images were acceptable and others stating that pictures of fully clothed people in public were inappropriate. Such vast differences in opinion call into question responses to the other survey questions about sexting.

Second, the researchers did not ask students if they themselves had ever produced, received, or forwarded sexual images. Instead, students were asked, "Have any of your friends shared intimate pictures/videos with a boyfriend or girlfriend (sometimes referred to as 'sexting')?" The researchers defended this targeting of friends rather than respondents by saying they felt respondents would be more open about a friend's practices than their own. However, it is conceivable that these 40% of students could have been referring to the same small group of friends that were known by their peers to be "sexters." This would mean that only a small fraction of the students were actually producing sexual images, which should have been the main concern.

The Pew Internet and American Life Project

In December of 2009, a study addressing sexting was conducted by researchers at the Pew Internet and American Life Project.

The sample included 800 teenagers age 12 to 17, the population of most concern given that sexual images produced by these youth could be considered child pornography.

Major Findings: Four percent of teens said they had sent a "sexually suggestive nude or nearly nude photo or video" of themselves to someone else via cell phone and only 15% of youth received such images (about one in seven teens).

Older teens were more likely to both send and receive sexual images (8% and 30% of 17-year-olds, respectively). In contrast, a much smaller percentage of 12-year-olds had "sexted" (4% sent and 4% received). Involvement in sexting was more likely among teens who used their cell phones on a regular basis, teens who had "unlimited" plans, teens who regularly used their phones to entertain themselves when they were bored, and teens who reported "always on" behavior, meaning that they did not turn off their phones except when they were required to. Teens were no more or less likely to engage in sexting if they knew their parents looked through their phones. However, teens were less likely to sext if their parents limited the overall number of messages the teens could receive.

Limitations: The study only addressed messages sent by cell phone, rather than including other digital means such as e-mail, instant messaging, and social networking sites. This could be a drawback of the study, since it leaves out many communication channels popular among teens. It also makes it difficult to compare the findings to those of the other studies that included a wider variety of communication channels. Like other studies, the phrase "nude or nearly nude" could have also been interpreted to mean photos of minors in underwear or bathing suits, which would not generally be illegal.

Drawing Conclusions

Recent media reports have given the impression that "sexting" is a problem of epidemic proportions among teenagers today.

However, analysis of the relevant research to date reveals that there is little consistency in the estimated prevalence of sexting among adolescents. In addition, the high estimates that have received the most media attention come from studies with a number of problems including unrepresentative samples, vaguely defined terms, and great potential for public misperception. Many otherwise valid findings have been presented by the media in ways that exaggerate the true extent of the problem. While sexting does seem to occur among a notable minority of adolescents, there is little reliable evidence that the problem is as far-reaching as many media reports have suggested. Although more conservative estimates do exist, these statistics are not as widely publicized.

Changes should be made to improve future studies on this topic. First, researchers should limit samples to only include minors (age 17 or younger) if they wish to address the primary concerns about youth-produced child pornography. While it may be interesting to study sexting rates among young adults, sexual images of this population are not illegal and should not be combined with estimates of sexting among minors.

Second, terminology should be consistent among studies, accurately reported by the media, and adequately explained to youth participants. Using terms such as "nude or nearly-nude images" may confuse teens participating in the studies and result in inaccurate estimates. It would also be best to focus only on images, not written exchanges, because sexual photographs of minors are illegal; sexual text messages between youth are generally not. If researchers used this standard terminology, more meaningful comparisons could be made between studies.

It is clear that a standardized definition of sexting is needed. Although sexting has become a popular term among the public, it has come to encompass too many activities to make it an appropriate term for formal research. Instead, the authors suggest using the term "youth-produced sexual images," defined as images created by minors (age 17 or younger) that depict minors and that are or could be considered child pornography under criminal statutes.

Third, there should be a greater emphasis on who these youth are sharing sexual images with and their reasons for doing this. While most media reports focus on youth sexting among peers, some youth may be sending sexual images to people they barely know, such as people they meet online. These online recipients could be adults who are pressuring teens into taking and sending the images. Most people would likely agree that these situations deserve more police attention.

Journalists and scholars seem eager to cite statistics about sexting, but this may be unwise due to the current lack of consistent findings and significant flaws in many studies. When citing the statistics, it is important to mention them in the context of other studies and also take into account the variety of circumstances that the term "sexting" can be used to describe. Until more reliable statistics are available, scholars and journalists should avoid citing the potentially inaccurate studies currently available. We suggest that journalists simply say: "there are no consistent and reliable findings at this time to estimate the true prevalence of the problem." At the very least, study findings should be presented in ways that do not exaggerate the problem or mislead readers. Writers should also clearly state what behaviors the statistics are referring to and not simply use the umbrella term of "sexting" to refer to the many different activities covered in the studies.

"When one considers the amount
of time an average teen spends on a
cell phone or the Internet, it is not
surprising that these technologies can
become tools of abuse."

Abusive Teen Dating Partners Use Technology as Tools of Abuse

Break the Cycle

Technology can become a tool of abuse in the hands of an abusive dating partner, argues the author of the following viewpoint. Abusers who seek to control and monitor their intimate partners use cell phones to constantly check in with and even spy on their partners, the author asserts. In addition, they claim, abusers use cell phones to harass and threaten victims and post unwanted images or information on social networking sites. Regrettably, many parents are unaware of the problem as teens fear that if they reveal the abuse, parents will invade their privacy or limit their access to technology. Break the Cycle works with teens to prevent and end domestic and dating violence.

As you read, consider the following questions:

1. According to Break the Cycle, how does the privacy offered by cell phones and the Internet pose a challenge to service providers?

2. In the author's view, what about some teens online social networking profiles makes them more vulnerable to abusive intimate partners?

3. What percentage of teens surveyed reported that a boyfriend or girlfriend made them afraid *not* to respond to an electronic message, as the author reports?

Today's teens are increasingly reliant upon technology in their everyday lives. Cell phones, PDAs [personal digital assistants], and the Internet provide teens with almost constant communication. While technology has greatly improved teens' ability to stay in touch with their friends, families, schools, and communities, these new technologies can also present a challenge to service providers who work with teens experiencing dating violence. In the hands of an abusive partner, the same tech devices and websites that connect teens can be turned into tools of abuse. The privacy offered by cell phones and the Internet adds another layer of challenge for providers, as this same privacy often means that high-tech abuse is hidden. Providers can help protect their teen clients by understanding the challenges that technology presents and sharing strategies for teens to stay safe.

Many teens use cell phones, email, social networking sites, and personal computers every day. A recent study found that 93% of teens use the Internet, 72% own a desktop computer, and 67% own cell phones; these numbers are increasing every year. More than half of 12 to 17 year olds who use the Internet have a profile on a social networking site such as Facebook or MySpace, and nearly half of teens visit a social networking site once or more times daily. Teens are using the Internet in every area of their lives and most report that the Internet and other digital devices make their lives easier.

Digitally Monitoring Dating Partners

When one considers the amount of time an average teen spends on a cell phone or the Internet, it is not surprising that these technologies can become tools of abuse in the hands of an abusive dating partner. While teens experience the same types of abuse as adults, the methods may be unique to teens and teen culture; the use of technology is one area where this is easily seen. The controlling behavior, or monitoring, that abusers often exercise over their partners is easy to translate to the digital world. Teen abusers can easily monitor their dating partners by frequently checking in by cell phone, text or instant messenger (IM) or by requiring a dating partner to check in. One in three teens say they are text messaged up to thirty times an hour by a partner or ex-partner inquiring where they are, what they are doing, or who they are with. Between cell phone calls and frequent texting, an abuser can exert almost constant control over a partner day and night.

Slightly more technologically savvy teens can spy on or monitor a partner through spyware programs or Global Positioning System (GPS) devices. Spyware is computer software, installed on a personal computer without the owner's knowledge, which can track internet usage, collect personal information, and intercept electronic communications. GPS-enabled cell phones can be accessed using online services to monitor the user's location, often without the user ever knowing.

However, one need not be a technophile to use the Internet to monitor a dating partner. Many teens post their schedule or location on their personal blogs, Facebook or MySpace pages. The list of people able to access this information is determined by the level of privacy that the teen has selected on his or her account. Many teens do not restrict access to the content that they post, including pictures. Recent reports show that 40% of teens make their online profile visible to anyone and 21% of teens do not restrict access to their photos. It can range from only those people on the teen's list of "friends" to anyone with an account to anyone at all, with no restrictions. Many teens post enough information to allow anyone with access to find them at any point during the day—cell phone number, class schedules, addresses, extracurricular activities, social events, and jobs. Even if the teen does not post personal information, it may be available on a friend's webpage or even a school website.

Digital Threats and Harassment

The potential for abuse through technology goes beyond mere monitoring to harassment, threats, and intimidation. One in four teens in a relationship has experienced harassment, name calling, or put downs from a current or former dating partner through cell phone or text messaging. And nearly one in five has been harassed or put down through a social networking site. An abuser can use his or her own webpage to post personal information or unwanted pictures about a dating partner. Teens who share their passwords with friends and dating partners risk having their own email accounts and webpages accessed and used by abusive dating partners. The speed of communication on the Internet allows this information to be shared among friends and classmates almost instantaneously, often before a teen even knows it has been posted.

Fear and intimidation through high-tech channels are just as real as any abuse in the non-digital world. Moreover, high-tech abuse does not happen in a vacuum. For many teens, threats or harassment via cell phone or the Internet merely reinforce the threats and verbal abuse they have experienced in person. In fact, 17% of teens in a recent survey report that a boyfriend or girlfriend has made them afraid to not respond to a cell phone call, email, IM, or text message because of what he or she might do.

Teens are talking about high-tech abuse and believe it is a serious problem for themselves and their peers. Approximately half of teens believe that computers and cell phones make abuse more likely to occur in a teen dating relationship and make it easier to conceal abuse from parents. Unfortunately, parents, teachers, and adult service providers are frequently in the dark about the abuse that occurs over cell phones and the Internet. Teens are unlikely to report any abuse, including high-tech abuse, to parents or other adults. The hidden nature of such abuse means that unless a teen reveals the abuse or an adult looks into the teen's computer or phone, it can easily go undetected. Sixty-seven percent of parents were unaware that their teens had dating partners check up on them thirty times a day on their cell phones and 82% of parents did not know that their teens were emailed or texted 30 times per hour. Monitoring via cell phone and text message often continues throughout the night, when teens are alone and parents are unaware of their teen's activities. Nearly one in four teens in a relationship communicated with their partner by cell phone or text messaging hourly between midnight and 5:00 A.M.

Tips for People Who Work with Teens

Changing your cell phone number. If your teen client is experiencing abuse from a current or former dating partner by cell phone, her first instinct might be to change the number. This might be the right approach for many teens, but it is important to first consider how your teen's abusive partner will respond to a disconnected phone number. If your teen is concerned that her partner may escalate the abuse in reaction to being unable to make contact, then changing your teen's phone number may actually do more harm than good. Further, by leaving the phone on and active, calls can be tracked by the phone company and text messages and voicemails saved for potential use in future legal cases. If your teen does decide to change her cell phone number, discuss strategies to keep the abusive partner from discovering the new number. Remind your teen to give the new number to the people in her support network—parents, close friends, and other service providers. If your teen is unsure about changing her cell phone number, discuss alternative methods of restricting contact from an abusive partner such as talking to the cell phone provider about call blocking and other features.

Google yourself. Encourage your teen clients to enter their names in websites such as Google, Flickr, and YouTube to see what information pops up. The amount of personal information contained in various websites can be surprising. Teens must know what information is available to someone looking for them on the Internet, including in cached websites, particularly if they wish to prevent a current or former dating partner from obtaining personal information such as phone number or address. If your teen client comes across a website that contains personal information he wishes to keep private, encourage him to contact the website host directly to see if they will remove the information.

Make your profile private. Talk to your teen clients about who has access to their Facebook or MySpace page and encourage them to make their profiles private. Both of these social networking sites allow users to determine who sees the information they post on their pages. Teens should be aware of how much they reveal about their contact information, class and work schedules, extracurricular activities, social events, and daily routines. This is especially true for a teen who has recently ended an abusive relationship or is trying to limit contact from an abusive dating partner. If your teen client has decided to change her phone number, email address, or has made other changes in her life, she should remind friends not post the new information on their own pages.

Check your computer. If you have teen clients who are experiencing abuse, encourage them to check their personal computers frequently for signs of tampering or spyware. Up to date spyware detection and antivirus software can help teens avoid computer tampering. Tell your teens to avoid using computers that their abusers have physical access to and to avoid opening suspicious email attachments, particularly electronic greeting cards, computer games, or anything that requires them to click a link. Suggest that they use a computer in a public location for communication with friends or any personal research, particularly if they are looking for resources on dating violence. If your teens suspect that someone has accessed their accounts, advise them to use a public computer to change the password to something that is not easy to guess. Finally, make sure your teen clients are familiar with the quick escape links that are common on domestic and dating violence online resources. These links allow a user to quickly navigate to another, innocuous website, such as Google or Yahoo if someone unexpectedly enters the room.

Preserve evidence. Most teens choose not to pursue legal remedies against abusive dating partners, and many cannot imagine ever changing their mind and deciding to go to court. Even so, it is important to encourage your teen clients to preserve any electronic communication that could be evidence in a legal case. Saving voicemails, text messages, and emails will arm them with the tools they will need if they do decide to pursue civil or criminal remedies in the future. And if they never decide to go to court, no harm was done. Voicemails can be recorded with a digital voice recorder; text messages and emails should be printed to avoid unintentional deletion. Any communication made on a website should be immediately printed because the content can be changed in an instant and the relevant piece of evidence lost.

Technology is not the enemy. Advances in technology have improved all of our lives and have allowed teens greater freedom and creativity than ever before. It is important to remember that although these tools can be manipulated by abusers, they are merely the tools of abuse; the underlying power and control remains the real problem. Dating violence will not be overcome by restricting access to technology but by teaching teens how to use it safely and productively. These same technologies offer service providers a tremendous opportunity to reach teens who are experiencing dating violence. Encourage your organization to offer online resources for teens, such as interactive educational materials, discussion boards, and email advice lines.

"*Both the new and traditional media are being used by adolescents as they learn more about their developing sexuality.*"

Media Have Both a Positive and Negative Impact on Teen Sexual Relationships

Jane D. Brown, Sarah Keller, and Susannah Stern

In the following viewpoint the authors assert that today's teens spend a lot of time using both traditional and digital media. Unfortunately, as a rule, neither promotes healthy sexuality, they argue. The sexual content on television often fails to depict the risks and responsibilities of sex, the authors claim. Moreover, they maintain, viewing Internet pornography can lead to gender stereotypes and casual sexual exploration. Some evidence shows that the Internet is a useful platform for gay and lesbian teens to seek like-minded teens; however, as a source of sexual health information, the Internet is underused, they conclude. Jane D. Brown, Sarah Keller, and Susannah Stern are communications professors at the University of North Carolina, Montana State University, and the University of San Diego, respectively.

Jane D. Brown, Sarah Keller, and Susannah Stern, "Sex, Sexuality, Sexting, and SexEd: Adolescents and the Media," *Prevention Researcher*, vol. 16, no. 4, November 2009, pp. 12–15.

As you read, consider the following questions:

1. According to Brown, Keller, and Stern, what are some of the factors that influence traditional media use and its effect on sexuality?
2. How may gay and lesbian youth use the Internet, in the authors' view?
3. What is one main concern with the use of new media to learn about sex and sexual health, in the authors' opinion?

Adolescents in the United States spend six to seven hours a day with some form of media, including television, music, movies, magazines, the Internet, and smart cell phones. These media have become important sex educators as they include frequent discussion and portrayals of sexual behavior that affect adolescents' conceptions of sexual attractiveness, romantic relationships, and sexual behavior. Here we summarize briefly what is known about the use, content and effects of sexual media among adolescents, consider how new media forms such as the Internet and cell phones are being used, and finally, discuss how the media can also be used to promote healthy sexual behavior. . . .

Traditional Media Use, Content, and Effects

Adolescents still spend a great deal of time each day using what we might call the "traditional" media—television, radio, movies, magazines. Much of the content in each of these media contains discussion and depictions of some aspect of sexuality and/or sexual behavior, although little of the content includes any mention or depiction of the possible risks or responsibilities of early, unprotected sexual behavior. Exposure to such content is related to sexual outcomes, ranging from body dissatisfaction, to earlier sexual intercourse, less contraceptive use, and even pregnancy.

Media use and effects on sexuality vary dramatically by a number of factors, including sexual maturity, gender, and race. Studies have shown, for example, that earlier maturing girls are more likely to be interested in sexual content in the media than their less physically mature agemates. One study found that of 150 television programs frequently viewed by early adolescents, only four were watched by more than one-third of both black and white adolescents. Girls and boys also differed dramatically in their most frequently watched television programs, with girls preferring more relationship-oriented shows and boys preferring sports and action-adventure.

The wide array of media available to teens provides the opportunity for choosing different kinds of content. Some apparently seek sexual content while others would rather not see it. [Researchers K.L.] L'Engle and [J.D. Brown, L.S. Romocki, and E. Donnerstein] identified four patterns of sexual media use among early adolescents (12 to 14 years old) which suggested that some teens also will be more susceptible to what they see about sex in the media than others, given their motivations and prior sexual experience. The teens they called "Virgin Valedictorians," for example, were the least interested in sexual media content and were focusing on doing well in school, while the "Sexual Sophisticates" preferred sexual content, including pornography, and were the most likely to have had sexual relationships.

Today most traditional media content is accessible on the Internet, and soon will be widely available 24/7 on handheld devices. Research on how teens are using such new media forms for learning about sex is just getting started, but some recent studies provide insight about trends.

New Media Use, Content, and Effects

The new media, also sometimes called digital media, include text messaging on cell phones, MP3 players (e.g., iPods), blogs or chat rooms on Web sites, and Internet social networking sites (SNS)

Adolescents' Use of New Media

Medium/ Channels	Use by Adolescents (12–17 years old)	Sexual Content
Internet	•Average 12.5 hours online per week •Are primarily online for email, IM/SNS, and gaming •30% of females, 70% of males view Internet porn	•Sexual health information available •Sexually explicit images/ pornography more accessible than ever before
Social Networking Sites (SNS)	•38% of tweens (12–14) and 77% of teens (15–17) have a SNS profile •SNS are especially popular among older females: 89% of 15- to 17-year-old girls have SNS	•Platform for sexual self-expression and finding like-minded teens (e.g., gay, abstinent) •About 1 in 10 teens are posting sexually suggestive images online
Cell Phones	•Have cell phone: 52% of 12–13 year olds 72% of 14–16 year olds 84% of 17 year olds •58% send text messages to friends (38% daily)	•Sexual health information available •About 1 in 5 teens are "sexting"

TAKEN FROM: Jane D. Brown, Sara Keller and Susannah Stern, "Sex, Sexuality, Sexting and Sex Ed: Adolescents and the Media," The Prevention Researcher, November 2009.

such as Facebook or MySpace, where many users can simultaneously create and communicate on the same Web pages. . . .

Adolescents are already using the new media to engage in activities relevant to sex and sexuality. However, those who speak sweepingly of the "dangers" or "promise" of the new media, oversimplify a dynamic and complex set of practices and potential effects.

Initial research suggests that adolescents, especially boys, are using pornography on the Internet. According to surveys of Dutch adolescents (12 to 17 years old) and young U.S. teens (12 to 14 years old), about 30% of females and 50 to 70% of males have viewed sexually explicit images online. Longitudinal studies have found that such exposure predicts less progressive gender role attitudes and perpetration of sexual harassment for males, and sexual uncertainty, uncommitted sexual exploration (i.e., one-night stands, hooking up), earlier oral sex and sexual intercourse for both males and females.

Adolescents also now have greater opportunity than ever before to present themselves publicly to a geographically disparate audience. Many young people choose to display information about their sexuality and sexual lives, such as by indicating their sexual orientations on their SNS profiles, posting stories and poems about sexual desire and experience on blogs, sharing naked or semi-naked pictures and videos of themselves on SNS profiles and via mobile phones ("sexting"), and discussing sexual practices on SNS and blogs. Recent studies (notably, none of which employed a true probability sample) indicate that between one-tenth to one-fifth of teens share "inappropriate" images, references to sexual activity, and/or naked or semi-naked pictures of themselves with others electronically.

Using Media for Sexual Self-Expression

Can the act of sharing such sexual content be beneficial for teens in any way? Many would say yes. In fact, it has been repeatedly argued that sexual self-expression on the Internet can be functional for adolescents. The Internet provides a relatively safe space for teens to explore and define themselves as sexual beings. Different forums offer distinct opportunities; for example, SNS allow users to craft themselves as sexual (or not-yet-sexual) people to their friends, compelling reflection on who they are and would like to be, and to initiate and maintain "dating" relationships that can seem more intimidating in the real world.

Research on gay and lesbian youth, in particular, has demonstrated the value of the Internet as a space for experimentation and self-definition that is often difficult or dangerous in offline spaces. On the Internet, GLBT [gay, lesbian, bisexual, transgender] youth discuss a variety of sexual identities and queer politics, as well as seek partners, navigate the coming out process, and frankly discuss sexual practices, including safer sex.

The Internet also allows those who have historically been discouraged from exploring or asserting sexual desire (especially adolescent girls) an opportunity to recognize their own agency by expressing such feelings openly. The type of validation they sometimes receive can empower young people to accept and assert agency in their own offline relationships. Communicating with unknown yet similar others can also be invaluable for adolescents in another way: via the Internet, young people with sexual health concerns or problems can find peers in similar circumstances whose empathy and companionship can provide life-saving emotional connection. For example, a teen experiencing emotional trauma who locates others in similar straits may feel less alone and overwhelmed, and thus be more inclined to engage in thoughtful reflection about his or her next steps.

The Risks of Sharing Sexual Content

There are, however, several legitimate concerns regarding teens' sharing of sexual content in the new media. One concern is that sexual content posted by teens may prompt the perception among teen viewers that sex is normal, even glamorous, and risk-free. Teens who see risky sexual practices that do not indicate negative consequences may be more likely to adopt the behaviors that are referenced. In consequence, [M.] Moreno [A. VanderStoep, M. Parks, F. Zimmerman, A. Kurth, and D. Christakis] suggest user-generated sexual content may also increase the pressure virginal teens feel to become sexually active.

Another concern is that young people, especially girls, who share provocative or sexual imagery of themselves engage in a form of self-objectification in which young people "learn to think of and treat their own bodies as objects of others' desires." In so doing, young people may "internalize an observer's perspective on their physical selves and learn to treat themselves as objects to be looked at and evaluated for their appearance" ([said the] American Psychological Association). The self-objectification involved in "sexting" has received scrutiny recently. Reputations are harmed, relationships broken, and friendships shattered when receivers of naked images violate senders' trust by sending the images on to others. Despite the growing moral panic surrounding sexting, [E.] Goodman suggested that "there is nothing particularly new about young people taking pictures of themselves. It's as old as the Polaroid. What's different now is that teenagers can be their own paparazzi and be vulnerable to the humiliation once reserved for celebrities." The ease of wide distribution also may increase the intensity and risks of such behavior.

The kinds of sexual content teens post on SNS may also affect how their friends and potential sexual partners treat them, likely in ways that reinforce the behaviors/identities presented. So, for example, a teen girl who presents herself as very sexual through a provocative picture and content indicating interest in sex may find herself labeled a "slut" by some and be more likely to encounter sexual solicitations. A recent study of teen girls who had been abused earlier in life found that those who created provocative avatars (an icon representing a person in cyberspace) were more likely to receive sexual solicitations from strangers.

Perhaps most worrisome is the possibility that the display or sexual content online increases teens' chances of online victimization. [J.] Wolak [D. Finkelhor, K. Mitchell, and M. Ybarra] have conducted a series of national studies that find that teens who send personal information or talk online to strangers about sex are at greatest risk for sexual victimization, since they are most likely to receive sexual solicitations. Other categories of teens who are known to be at greater risk include those with histories of sexual abuse, sexual orientation concerns, and patterns of off- and online risk taking. Teens who respond to sexual solicitations are at risk not only for predation, but also for potential illness. Studies show that sex partners who meet online engage in higher-risk sexual behaviors, and are therefore at higher risk of acquiring sexually transmitted illnesses, than do partners who meet through conventional means.

New Media as Sexual Health Educators

The newest forms of media also offer a variety of strategies for getting sexual health information to youth. New media can be successful channels for sex education for precisely the same reasons that youth are such avid users. Young people use digital media for exploring and maintaining social, sexual, and romantic relationships because of presumed safety, perceived anonymity, transcendence from adult control, 24/7 availability, and the ability to communicate with peers.

Young audiences are frequent users of new media for sexual health information. Hundreds, if not thousands, of sexual health sites are maintained online, and studies show that about a quarter or more of online teens access the Internet to find information about sex, sexually transmitted diseases, and pregnancy. Sites like www.iwannaknow.org provide interactive games that may foster safe sex negotiation. In one study, 41% of young adults said they had changed their behavior because of health information they found online, and almost half had contacted a health care provider as a result.

Most teens (and youth advocates) agree that the Internet is a valuable place to turn for answers to embarrassing sex-related questions, to learn more about uncomfortable topics, to familiarize themselves with intimate body parts, and to gain perspective on conditions and sexual practices. Sexual health Web sites can also provide ideas about how to handle sexual situations, how to use birth control, and how to seek help when needed. Online sources may offer a sense of anonymity that may encourage teenagers to ask questions they would feel uncomfortable asking in person.

There are two main concerns associated with the use of new media to learn about sex and sexual health. First is the possibility that the information teens access and/or receive is inaccurate or misleading. Since adolescents have shown little proclivity to assess the credibility of Web sites (basing their assessments on how "professional" sites look rather than on who built the site and why), it seems reasonable to speculate that teens searching online may receive information that misinforms them, or is misinterpreted by them, potentially to their detriment. This may especially be the case when Web sites created for teens primarily or exclusively use medical terminology to refer to anatomy, sexual practices, and conditions. In particular, teens who have poor health literacy (who are also more likely to be at risk for sexually transmitted diseases), are more likely to search for sexual health information using slang terms, which may lead to less credible Web sites. Furthermore, the several content analyses that have looked at safe sex Web site design have found that sites promote condom use and abstinence, but few discuss other safe sex strategies, such as reducing the number of partners, reducing casual sex, or delaying first intercourse.

A second concern associated with the use of new media to learn about sex and sexual health is that teens who turn to the Internet for answers may turn away from real people in their lives. Parents, community members, teachers, and doctors from teens' own communities may better understand the unique needs and situations of individual teens. Moreover, many adults feel a strong desire to communicate certain values about sex to their own teens and dislike the notion that strangers (whether they be Web site creators or senders of sex-ed text messages) might promote or at least not condemn sexual thoughts and activities among teens. . . .

It is clear that both the new and traditional media are being used by adolescents as they learn more about their developing sexuality. Much of existing media content, unfortunately, is not designed to result in healthy sexuality. Both new and older forms of media can be used to promote healthier sexuality among adolescents, however. Certainly we need to know more—both in terms of the types of interventions possible with traditional and new media, and from evaluations to ensure that time and funds are well spent.

"Adults who work with teens should consider viewing and discussing episodes of [reality television shows about teen pregnancy] in their activities or programs that are designed to help reduce teen pregnancy."

Reality Television Shows Reveal the Risks of Teen Pregnancy

Katherine Suellentrop, Jane Brown, and Rebecca Ortiz

A study from the National Campaign to Prevent Teen and Unplanned Pregnancy reveals that reality television shows about teen pregnancy can influence teens' perceptions, claims the authors of the following viewpoint. Although teen pregnancy reality shows paint a glamorous picture of teen pregnancy for some, these shows create an opportunity to talk to teens about the risks of sex. Katherine Suellentrop conducts research at the National Campaign to Prevent Teen and Unplanned Pregnancy, Jane Brown is a communications professor at the University of North Carolina, and Rebecca Ortiz is a graduate student there.

Katherine Suellentrop, Jane Brown, and Rebecca Ortiz, "Evaluating the Impact of MTV's 16 and Pregnant on Teen Viewers' Attitudes About Teen Pregnancy," *Science Says*, vol. 45, October 2010, pp. 1–4. Copyright © 2010 by The National Campaign to Prevent Teen and Unplanned Pregnancy. All rights reserved. Reproduced by permission..

As you read, consider the following questions:

1. Why are Suellentrop, Brown, and Ortiz interested in exploring whether media might help prevent teen pregnancy?
2. What do the authors believe is the critical distinction between television shows such as *16 and Pregnant* and teen pregnancy prevention programs?
3. In the authors' view, what were some of the differences between boys' and girls' opinions found in the study by the National Campaign to Prevent Teen and Unplanned Pregnancy?

Concerns exist about the sexual content in popular media and the influence these images and messages might have on young people's sexual behavior. Sexual content in the media has increased over the past several decades, and research has found that the sexual content in media can influence teens' *attitudes* about sex and contraception and may also influence their sexual *behavior*. In fact, research has documented an association between exposure to sexual content on television and teen pregnancy.

Little research, however, has been conducted to better understand how media might also have positive effects by, for example, decreasing risky sexual behavior and promoting healthier decisions among teens. Given that teens' use of media has increased over the past decade, and that the amount of sexual content in the media has also increased, it is reasonable to explore whether media might be used to help prevent teen pregnancy.

This *Science Says* presents results from an evaluation study designed to learn more about how watching and discussing episodes of the popular MTV documentary-style reality show *16 and Pregnant* influences teens' perceptions of getting pregnant and becoming a parent at a young age. The document also includes new public opinion data that shed light on teens' perceptions of *16 and Pregnant*, in particular, and their views about how media might influence teens' decisions about sex more generally. Complete results from this new public opinion survey of both teens and adults will be available soon in a [National Campaign to Prevent Teen and Unplanned Pregnancy] report entitled *With One Voice 2010*.

About the Evaluation

The National Campaign worked with innovation, Research, and Training, Inc. (iRT) to learn more about teens' perceptions of the show *16 and Pregnant*, and whether or not watching and discussing the show affected their attitudes about teen pregnancy. In partnership with the Boys and Girls Clubs of America, 18 clubs in one southern state participated in this research study. The clubs were randomly assigned to either see the episodes (treatment = nine clubs) or not (control = nine clubs). All participants obtained parental consent and completed questionnaires at baseline and again a week later. Teens in the treatment groups viewed three episodes of the first-season of *16 and Pregnant* (the Maci, Amber, and Ebony episodes). Boys and Girls Club members watched one episode per day and the episodes were shown in different orders at different clubs. A group leader led a discussion of the shows with the teens each day. Control group teens did not view or discuss the episodes at the clubs, but did complete the pre- and post-test questionnaires.

A total of 162 teens participated and completed both the pre- and post-test questionnaires (78 from the control group and 84 from the treatment group). The average age of the participants was 13.5 years, ranging from 10 to 19 years old. Most participants were female (62%), and three-quarters (75%) were African American. Nearly three-quarters of all participants (73%) received reduced or free lunch at school. About one-third (34%) of the participants reported having had sex.

Television Shows vs. Prevention Programs

Television and other media alone do not cause—and cannot prevent—teen pregnancy. However, entertainment media can reach millions of teens with important messages about teen pregnancy. It is important to note that there is a critical distinction between this evaluation—which attempts to understand teens' views about teen pregnancy as a result of watching and discussing MTV's *16 and Pregnant*—versus an impact evaluation of a prevention program whose sole purpose is to reduce teen pregnancy. While evidence-based teen pregnancy prevention programs are guided by specific behavioral theories and have the explicit goal of changing behavior to reduce risk of teen pregnancy, television shows such as *16 and Pregnant* are created for entertainment with the goal of attracting viewers and keeping them engaged.

- *16 and Pregnant* got teens talking and thinking about teen pregnancy. The majority of teens who watched and discussed the show in a group also later talked to a friend about the show. More than one-third—40%—talked to a parent afterward and about one-third spoke to a sibling or girlfriend/boyfriend. Clearly, this show is an excellent conversation-starter for teens.

- The more teens talked about the show, the less likely they were to think that teen pregnancy and teen parenthood are commonplace, or to agree with the statement, "most teens want to get pregnant." Parents and practitioners should be encouraged to talk about this show (and others like it) to the teens in their lives to help ensure that these young people know what the adults in their lives think about these shows and their messages.

- The teens in this study enjoyed watching and discussing the *16 and Pregnant* episodes and thought that the show was realistic. Neither the boys nor girls who watched the episodes wanted to imitate the teens in the episodes they watched. In fact, nearly all teens (93%) who watched the show agreed (53% strongly agreed) with the statement: "I learned that teen parenthood is harder than I imagined from these episodes." Although some have claimed that the show "glamorizes" teen pregnancy, the findings from this evaluation and the polling data noted above show that teens do not share that view.

Teens' Opinions Differ by Gender

A number of other findings emerged from this study. Analysis of the pre- and post-test questionnaires determined that regardless of whether or not they watched the episodes, girls had more realistic expectations than boys did about teen parenthood. In particular, many girls felt that becoming a teen parent would make it hard for them to finish high school to attend college, and to achieve future career goals. Research shows that fewer than four in ten mothers who have a child before they turn 18 earn a high school diploma by age 22. Overall, girls disagreed more strongly than boys with the notion that becoming a teen parent would help to get their lives on track. Teen boys were less likely than the girls to believe that teen parenthood would have a negative impact on their educational or career goals.

In addition, teens who saw and discussed the episodes reported that they enjoyed watching and talking about the show and that they learned something new from doing so. The more they liked it, the more likely they were to have negative views about teen pregnancy.

Teens were eager to recommend the show to others; 89% of participants agreed (56% of those strongly agreed) with the statement: "I think all teenagers should watch a show like this." Many said they would recommend that friends participate in the discussion, too.

A Cautionary Note

A few findings from the evaluation suggest that viewing *16 and Pregnant* could have an undesirable effect on some viewers. More specifically, teens who watched and discussed the episodes were more likely to believe that teens do want to get pregnant compared to those in the group who did not watch or discuss the

Teens' Perspectives on Pregnancy in TV Shows

New polling data, from a nationally representative survey com-missioned by the National Campaign [to Prevent Teen and Un-planned Pregnancy], asked teens their opinions on media and teen pregnancy and their views about 16 and Pregnant. *Find-ings from young people ages 12–19 include:*

- Six in ten teens have watched at least some of *16 and Pregnant.*
- Among those teens who have watched the show, 82% think that the show helps teens better understand the challenges of teen pregnancy and parenthood, compared to 15% who believe that it glamorizes teen pregnancy.
- In addition, the clear majority of teen boys (67%) and girls (79%) agree with the statement, "when a TV show or char-acter I like deals with teen pregnancy, it makes me think more about my own risk (of becoming pregnant/causing a pregnancy) and how to avoid it."

Katherine Suellentrop, Jane Brown, and Rebecca Ortiz, "Evaluating the Impact of MTV's 16 and Pregnant *on Teen Viewers' Attitudes About Teen Pregnancy," National Campaign to Prevent Teen and Unplanned Pregnancy,* Science Says, *no. 45, October 2010.*

episodes. Note that discussing the episodes later with a friend seemed to moderate this finding somewhat. Also, among teens who had never had sex, those who viewed and discussed the episodes were more likely than those who had [had sex] not to believe that most teens want to get pregnant, and that if they were to get pregnant or cause a pregnancy, that they "will be with the baby's mother/father forever."

In addition, regardless of whether they watched and discussed the episodes or not, sexually experienced teens were more likely than those teens who had not had sex to think that if they became a teen parent, their parents would help them raise the baby. Sexually experienced teens were also more likely to believe that people would view them as more mature if they had a child as a teen.

These types of shows reach a large number of teens and can be used in a positive way. The results of this project clearly support the idea that teens are interested in watching and discussing reality television shows about teen pregnancy, and that messages about the realities of teen pregnancy and parenting in these shows can influence teens' attitudes about the challenges of teen parenthood. Given the popularity of these shows, their messages clearly reach a large number of teens. For all these reasons, adults who work with teens should consider viewing and discussing episodes of such shows in their activities or programs that are designed to help reduce teen pregnancy and/or foster positive youth development more broadly.

| "*MTV's message of safe sex and education is lost among the glittering lights of the paparazzi, booking agents, and nice paydays.*"

Reality Television Shows Glamorize Teen Pregnancy

Susie Kroll

While reality television shows about teen pregnancy successfully illustrate the challenges of teen motherhood, when teen moms become celebrities, the message to avoid teen pregnancy is lost, argues the author of the following viewpoint. When the teen moms on the show appear in tabloid newspapers, television interviews, and with other celebrities, this glittering Hollywood world will tempt some teens who have few options, she asserts. More troubling, the author claims, these programs televise horrific instances of verbal and physical abuse—violence that is not worth the price of temporary fame and fortune. Susie Kroll is a teen dating violence and healthy relationship educator.

As you read, consider the following questions:

1. What factors does Kroll think may have influenced whether the attitudes and behaviors of the people appearing on the shows were real?

2. Who does the author say delivered some of the most horrible and abusive verbal violence that she has witnessed on TV?

3. Why would supermarket tabloids pay for interviews and photos of reality TV teen moms rather than other celebrities, in the author's view?

Teen Mom and *16 and Pregnant* are weekly series on MTV. MTV camera crews follow the pregnancy and first years of life of a teenage mother. In the beginning, I watched the show due to its popularity with my target audience of teens. The crew left little to the viewer's imagination when it came to all of the irritations, pains, relationship drama, parental drama, and birthing process. The viewers got to see how these young girls learned to or didn't learn to cope with the seriousness of becoming a teen mom.

The Good

There were angry parents, sad parents, and even parents that were very celebratory of the impending newborn. Though I had to wonder how much of it was because the cameras were with them 24/7, how much was scripted, and how much [was] truly the chaos that existed in each family. MTV made no secret of how hard labor was, how each teen and sometimes the baby's father struggled with money, and even how as new parents these teens couldn't let go of their teen mentality and step up to the plate of responsibility.

If I were a teen watching this show, I would be thinking to myself, "I am never going to have unprotected sex." I would also be thinking, "Labor looks like it sucks." Finally, I would think, "I am way too into myself and what I want to even consider having a kid at 16 or so." So, the Good, MTV does a pretty good job of portraying the hardships that a teen mom may face. There was no shortage of financial difficulty, parental judgment, and baby daddy drama. The series makes teen pregnancy look pretty unappealing.

The Bad

Unfortunately, there is also no shortage of domestic violence, teen dating violence, verbal abuse, and child neglect. One teen mom in particular has been charged with multiple counts of domestic violence against her baby's father. She was shown, on the series, punching and hitting her baby's father. She even attempted to kick him down the stairs, all while their little girl of 2 watched. Another teen mom slapped her boyfriend on the face. Still another received verbally abusive texts and voicemails from the father of her baby, whom later in the series she decided to let move in with her and the baby. The abuse is not solely between the teen mothers and their baby's fathers. Sadly, one teen mom endured some of the most horrible and abusive verbal violence from her own mother. This teen mom struggled to be the daughter that her mom could love by cleaning their house, trying to shop with her mom, and even reaching out to her with heart-felt dialog. She was met with some of the most awful, hurtful, and damaging verbal abuse I have ever seen aired on national TV.

So the Bad, MTV crews filmed horrible verbal and physical abuse. MTV did do follow up shows with Dr. Drew Pinsky that touched on the violence on the show and talked with the teen moms, abusers, and fathers. I think it did little to detract from the violence. All of the follow up specials were overshadowed by the filmed violence and other parts of the series. I believe it wasn't handled as deeply as it needed to be to show viewers the seriousness and unacceptability of the incidents.

The Ugly

If the purpose of creating shows like *Teen Mom* and *16 and Pregnant* were to dissuade teens from becoming just that, teen moms, I believe in the beginning they would have been successful. The

But I Am Studying Cartoon. © Copyright 2006, by Chris Slane and Cagle Cartoons.com.

series showed, to the best of its ability, the ups, downs, and struggles of becoming a teen parent. MTV illustrated the loss of friends, personal time, sleep, a childhood, money, relationships, and even not graduating from high school very clearly. Regrettably, these shows had huge side effects. The public demanded to know more. We didn't want to end with these girls saying they wish they would have waited to become parents. No, we wanted to see what happened next, who they ended up with, how the babies were doing, and if certain situations resolved themselves. This created a media frenzy. These girls became celebrities in what seemed to be overnight.

Their faces were plastered all over the supermarket tabloids (and still continue to be). After all, it is cheaper for these magazines to pay for interviews and photos of these teen moms than say the Reese Witherspoons and Angelina Jolies of the world. Suddenly, these girls are rubbing elbows with Bristol Palin and other celebrities. They are having what looks to be storybook weddings immortalized in tabloids with beautiful dresses and flowers. Many of these teen moms are living their 15 minutes of fame out right now. They have booking agents, are writing books, modeling, booking interviews and photo shoots, and even competing the spots on *Dancing with the Stars*.

So, the Ugly, if I was a teen and I was seeing this, unexpectedly, teen pregnancy looks pretty glamorous. If I wanted to be famous, get rich, and be on TV, now I have been given a road map to see if I can make it happen. If I was faced with single parenthood, welfare, no education, and life in a small town, the shining lights of MTV and Hollywood would be too tempting to pass up. Suddenly, the hardships don't look so hard.

MTV's message of safe sex and education is lost among the glittering lights of the paparazzi, booking agents, and nice paydays. Even more so, the violence, domestic, teen, and verbal are completely lost in the flurry of makeup artists, TV interviews, and Hollywood glitz. I completely disagree with making domestic and teen dating violence look like a small price to pay for fame, fortune, and forgetting about the most important thing, the babies.

"Media literacy has great promise for sex education by providing adolescents with the cognitive framework necessary to understand and resist the influences of media on their decision making concerning sex."

Media Literacy Programs Help Teens Resist Negative Media Images of Teen Relationships

Bruce E. Pinkleton, Erica Weintraub Austin, Marilyn Cohen, Yi-Chun "Yvonnes" Chen, and Erin Fitzgerald

Because teens spend hours consuming media saturated with sexual content, media literacy programs serve as an effective sex education tool, claim the authors of the following viewpoint. Although misleading media portrayals of teen sex influence teen attitudes and behavior, media literacy programs teach participants how media use sexual imagery to achieve their own goals, the authors argue. Bruce E. Pinkleton and Erica Weintraub Austin are communications professors at Washington State University; Marilyn

Bruce E. Pinkleton, Erica Weintraub Austin, Marilyn Cohen, Yi-Chun "Yvonnes" Chen, and Erin Fitzgerald, "Effects of a Peer-Led Media Literacy Curriculum on Adolescents' Knowledge and Attitudes Toward Sexual Behavior and Medial Portrayals of Sex," *Health Communication*, vol. 23, 2008, pp. 462–65, 469–70. Copyright © 2008 by Taylor and Francis. All rights reserved. Reproduced by permission.

Cohen is an education professor at the University of Washington; Yi-Chun "Yvonnes" Chen is a communications professor at Virginia Tech; and Erin Fitzgerald, at the time of writing, worked at the Northwest Center for Excellence in Media Literacy at the University of Washington.

As you read, consider the following questions:

1. According to the authors, how much time do teens spend watching TV?
2. What do the authors say is the primary strength of media literacy training?
3. What is the impact of gender on media literacy programs, in the authors' view?

Mediated sexual portrayals and their consequences for teen health are of increasing concern to health communication specialists, educators, and researchers. Each year approximately 4 million adolescents contract a sexually transmitted disease. In addition, approximately 34% of women under the age of 20 become pregnant, accounting for about one fourth of all unintended pregnancies. The teenage birth rate in the United States is the highest in the Western industrialized world, costing a minimum of $7 billion every year.

Adolescents spend an average of 8 hours a day consuming mass media, of which 3 to 4 hours each day is devoted to watching TV. Research indicates that sexual content and related portrayals dominate television programming content, including those programs popular with adolescents. Because TV plays such an important role in the lives of adolescents, research results indicate it is an important and frequently used source of sexual information, along with parents and peers. Nevertheless, when asked to think about role models on TV that promote healthy decision making regarding sex, 86% of teens are unable to name any.

Responding to Teen Pregnancy

Even though the teenage pregnancy rate has declined for the past several years, adolescents in the United States have higher pregnancy and birth rates, lower rates of contraceptive use, and higher rates of sexually transmitted infections than do adolescents in other developed countries, including Great Britain, Australia, France, and Germany. One response of the federal government has been to fund abstinence-only sex education programs. Federal definitions of abstinence-only education include teaching young people that social, psychological, and physical benefits accrue when they refrain from sexual activity.

Researchers' have expressed concerns that abstinence-only messages are inadequate from a comprehensive sex education perspective, and research findings are inconclusive concerning their effectiveness. Given these concerns, the purpose of this study was to evaluate the efficacy of a peer-led, media literacy program concerning sexual abstinence. The program, developed by the Experimental Education Unit at the University of Washington, uses media literacy to communicate information regarding abstinence and sexual health to young people. The evaluation is based on participants' understanding of media and on their decision-making processes, and provides an evidence-based test of the effectiveness of the program as a catalyst for better decision making about sexual behavior.

Sex in the Media

The prevalence of sexual portrayals in the mass media provides adolescents with numerous, often misleading, sexual depictions ranging from kissing and flirting to relatively explicit portrayals of sexual intercourse. Sexual depictions are so common that adolescents encounter in the range of 10,000 to 15,000 sexual references or jokes and instances of nudity in the media each year. Sex-related scenes appear on television at an average rate of 4.6 per hour and the amount of sexual content on television has increased from 56% in 1998 to approximately 70% in 2005.

Meanwhile, nearly 90% of the television programs containing risky sexual behaviors fail to provide any information concerning risks or responsibilities associated with sex, and only 4% of programs popular with adolescents mention any risk or responsibility related to sexual behavior.

Researchers note that media portrayals generally provide little information about sexual health and tend to promote sexual stereotypes. Content analyses reveal that television programs commonly provide glamorized, unrealistic portrayals of sex and portray sexual intercourse as a leisure activity, for example. According to a content analysis of the 15 most popular teen shows, 75% of characters who engaged in sexual activity commonly experienced positive outcomes as a result of their sexual experience. [J.D.] Brown and [J.R.] Steele note that adolescents are more likely to emulate the portrayed sexual behaviors when they perceive that characters on TV rarely suffer from negative consequences of unprotected sexual behavior.

TV and Teen Sexual Attitudes

Research results consistently show an association between television viewing and adolescents' sexual attitudes and behaviors. Nearly three of every four 15- to 17-year-old adolescents report that TV makes sexual behavior seem normative among adolescents and influences other teenagers' sexual behavior, and one fourth report that sexual television programs directly influence their own.

Adolescents' exposure to sexual television content associates with their initiation of sexual behavior. Research by [L.M.] Ward and [K.] Friedman indicates, for example, that exposure to sexual content and higher identification with popular TV characters associates with higher levels of high school students' actual sexual experience. The results of longitudinal research indicate that viewing sexual activity on television affects 12- to 17-year-olds' sex-related attitudes and behaviors even a year later. Additional research results concerning media exposure and sexual behavior conducted by [J.D.] Brown [K.L. L'Engle, C.J. Pardun, G. Guo,

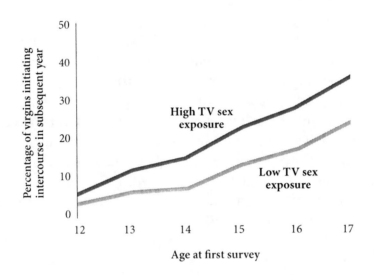

Television and Teen Sex

Across all age groups, teens who saw the most sex on television were twice as likely to initiate intercourse within the next year as were those who saw the least.

High TV sex exposure

Low TV sex exposure

Age at first survey

Percentage of virgins initiating intercourse in subsequent year

TAKEN FROM: RAND Corporation, "Does Watching Sex on Television Influence Teens' Sexual Activity?," *RAND Health Research Highlights*, 2004.

K. Kennery, and C. Jackson] reveal that a strong association exists between sexual content in the mass media and adolescents' self-reported sexual experiences 2 years later.

Adolescent Sex Education

There are a number of approaches to reducing adolescent sexual activity and its consequences, including unintended pregnancies and the spread of sexually transmitted infections. Despite generally strong public support for such programs, however, the specific nature of programs depends on the social and political context in which they are developed and delivered; these can affect program quality and outcomes. Most youth receive some form of sex or HIV-prevention education when they are in school, for example, but teachers may omit important topics. As a result, although a variety of programs have positive effects on variables related to a reduction in adolescent sexual activity, research results indicate that only some programs successfully delay the onset of sexual activity or increase contraceptive use. . . .

The ubiquitous nature of sexual content in the media and the primacy of the media as a source of sexual information for adolescents raise the potential for the media to serve as a catalyst for sex education programming. In general, scholars define media literacy broadly in terms of a person's ability to access, analyze, evaluate, and communicate messages in a wide variety of forms. As the field has developed, educators and others typically have focused on teaching young people the process of critically analyzing and learning to create media messages. A variety of media literacy curricula exist with little standardization regarding approaches and applications. Regardless of differences in perspective and approaches to media literacy education, the common goals of most curricula include helping young people become informed, active participants in the communication process rather than passive message targets. . . .

Evaluating Media Literacy Programs

Portrayals of sex in the media and their consequences for teen health are of significant concern to health professionals. Misleading sexual portrayals in the mass media are common; experts estimate that adolescents are exposed to 14,000 messages concerning sex each year. The purpose of this study was to evaluate a peer-led program that used media literacy to communicate information regarding abstinence and sexual health to young people. This evaluation, based on participants' understanding of the media and their decision-making processes, demonstrated positive results on all tested outcomes. Study results indicated that adolescents receiving the training were less likely to over-estimate the extent to which teens are sexually active, more likely to think they could delay becoming sexually active, less likely to expect that having sex would provide social benefits, more aware of myths about sex, and less likely to consider sexual media imagery desirable.

Study participants showed unambiguous enthusiasm for the lessons, with 85% rating the program as better than other sex education programs in which they had participated. They also demonstrated good recall of lesson material, which focused primarily on societal norms rather than on medical information. Given the message restrictions required of this curriculum, research evidence suggests that this program alone is unlikely to provide sufficient sex education to students, consistent with the position taken by the Society for Adolescent Medicine and based on the evidence-based criteria for successful programs developed by [D.] Kirby. Nevertheless, because participants reported that the lessons made them think and taught them something new, the results suggest that media literacy may successfully encourage the development of critical thinking skills among young people, at least concerning sex and the media. Although researchers measured only participants' perceptions in this study, the increase in young people's efficacy should give them a stronger sense of their ability to positively control their sexual health and to resist the peer pressure associated with sexual activity among teens. Research has shown that efficacy is one of the most important determinants of health-related decisions. A critical outcome for sex education programs, efficacy commonly enjoys a strong link to behavior.

These results suggest that a primary strength of media literacy training is its ability to strip away the facade concerning sex that media provide to young people. Participants come away with a less-idealized and more fact-based understanding of how media operate and the ways in which media outlets use sex and sexual imagery to promote their own ends, such as increased viewership or readership. Based on the results of this study, this critical media perspective and enhanced understanding appear likely to have a positive influence on adolescents' decision making regarding sexual behavior.

Another benefit of media literacy programs may be their ability to reach program participants regardless of gender. Gender differences did not interfere with lesson effectiveness in this study, although in terms of understanding the media's influence on adolescents' sexual behavior, boys may have learned more from the media literacy lessons than girls did. The results of other evaluations of media literacy curricula have indicated that these programs may successfully influence different audiences when they are tailored to meet the varying needs of each group. This suggests that media literacy may provide a flexible tool for reaching multiple target audiences.

Addressing Limitations

As a post-test-only quasi-experiment, it is not possible to generalize this study's results. This study employed a purposive sample without random assignment and employed only one set of media literacy lessons. As a result, it is not possible to pinpoint the specific aspects of the lesson strategies and implementation responsible for the positive results obtained in this trial. To determine that a typical media literacy program can accomplish the outcomes demonstrated in this evaluation would require random assignment to a representative variety of curricula. In addition, readers should interpret the gender-related finding with care given the nature of this study. Adolescent decision making regarding sexual abstinence is a complicated process and researchers should conduct additional studies to confirm or disconfirm gender-based outcomes in an effort to better understand this process. In future research, it would be useful to perform an evaluation with a pretest–post-test design, including random assignment to conditions and delayed post-tests measuring actual behavior.

Even with these limitations, the results of this study suggest that media literacy has great promise for sex education by providing adolescents with the cognitive framework necessary to understand and resist the influences of media on their decision making concerning sex. Because sexual imagery is such a common part of media messages, there seems to be an almost intuitive link between sex and media. Educators can take advantage of this link in communicating health-based information to adolescents. This link may allow media literacy–based sex education to seem relevant and useful to its audience, for example. Because adults tend to believe that media comprise an important information source for adolescents and commonly express concerns about sexualized media imagery, a media literacy–based curriculum also may be well received by a broad spectrum of parents. Finally, the results of this study demonstrate how peers can exert positive influences on each other and indicate that a peer-led media literacy curriculum might provide more general benefits for adolescents that go beyond the content of the curriculum.

"Carefully preparing children for the . . . endless assault of peer pressure, media glorification of irresponsible sexuality, and advertising come-ons is the only way to create a sense of security for parents and children alike."

Parents Must Mediate Negative Images of Teen Dating in the Media

Keith Ferrell

Mass and digital media images that glorify irresponsible sex constantly bombard American teens, claims the author of the following viewpoint. Parents must counter these messages, he argues, and help children develop a healthy sexuality. Letting teens know that they have the power to resist media and peer pressure is crucial, the author asserts. The most important step, however, is to teach sexual responsibility so that teens can avoid the risks that come from bad judgments, he maintains. Nevertheless, Ferrell reasons, parents must keep the communication lines open and ensure their children know that they are loved despite their decisions. Keith Ferrell is a contributing writer to Healthy Children, *a publication of the American Academy of Pediatrics.*

As you read, consider the following questions:

1. What does Dr. Charles R. Wibbelsman say is critical about the conversation parents have with their children?

2. When does the author say it is the right time for parents to start taking about sex with a child?

3. What does Dr. Wibbelsman say parents should avoid when answering the wholly natural questions teens have about sex and sexual identity?

Adolescence can be tough enough to get through without questions of sex, sexuality, and sexual identity. But adolescents are humans, too—no matter how alien they may seem to their parents at times. Openly addressing the all-too-human questions of sexual development, sexual desire, and the nature of the adolescent's developing sexual identity are critical. Sharing factual information with and giving good moral guidance . . . is a vitally important part of helping [a] teen understand herself or himself. It can help [teens] avoid devastating, and possibly life-threatening, errors in judgment.

"Above all, it is critical that parents be truthful, honest, and available to their children," says Charles R. Wibbelsman, M.D., FAAP, Chief of Adolescent Medicine at Kaiser Permanente in San Francisco and a member of the American Academy of Pediatrics' Committee on Adolescence.

"Parents often have their own agenda—don't do this and don't do that. But they need to take a step back and leave the judgments aside for this discussion," says Warren Seigel, M.D., FAAP, Chairman of the Pediatrics Department and Director of Adolescent Medicine at Coney Island Hospital, Brooklyn, N.Y. "The most appropriate and important thing for a parent and a child or adolescent in dealing with questions about sexuality and sexual health is an open channel of communication."

The Messages They Get

In today's hyper-sexualized culture of Internet sites, mass media entertainers, and 24/7 programming, the traditional "birds and bees" lecture (or pamphlet handed to the child to read on her or his own) on reproductive basics is completely inadequate. Carefully preparing children for the normal changes in their bodies as well as the endless assault of peer pressure, media glorification of irresponsible sexuality, and advertising come-ons is the only way to create a sense of security for parents and children alike.

"There are a lot of things in the media that are not appropriate for a particular age," says Dr. Wibbelsman, who is co-author of *The Teenage Body Book* and *Growing and Changing*. "We don't put children on the street and wish them luck before sending them out on their own. We hold their hands. We educate them about the risks. And we trust them with increasing responsibility only as they're old enough and show they're ready to handle it."

"The media particularly and everything around us talks about sex," adds Dr. Seigel. "It's hard to avoid it."

The only foolproof approach to sexual safety, of course, is to say "no" and defer sexual activity until later in life. The good news is that as many as half of all adolescents do just that. But that leaves the other half at risk—many of them engaging in unprotected sex, exposing themselves to potentially grave disease and unwanted pregnancy.

"The most important thing to teach your child is responsibility," Dr. Seigel says. "Discuss how to make decisions and understand what the consequences of decisions will be. You can start by discussing decisions and consequences that don't involve sex, and then move the conversation toward sexuality. After all, there are consequences to having sex or not having sex, and every child is going to get a lot of misinformation along the way from their peers and the media."

The pressures upon children—from peers and also the media as mentioned above—may actually offer one of the most effective pathways to opening what must be an ongoing dialogue about

D-A-Y-C-A-R-E Shadows Cartoon. © Copyright 2011, by JD Crowe and Cagle Cartoons.com.

sex and sexuality, not a single talk or lecture. What to do, then? It's good to turn these encounters with the media into teachable moments.

"Seeing something in the media that is obviously sexually charged can be a springboard for conversation between adolescent and parent," says Dr. Wibbelsman. "Is the ad bad or good? What's the ad trying to say? Use this moment as an opportunity to teach and encourage, not to pronounce a harsh, dismissive judgment. By engaging the child and building his self-esteem and her confidence in her ability to make judgments, you're showing him that you respect what he's learning and how she's growing in her decision-making."

After all, however adult their appearance, behavior, and attitudes may appear, adolescents remain closer to childhood than adulthood, and children need ongoing parental guidance to prepare for adulthood. "I know it's a lot of work, but parents need to monitor what their children see and be there, available to them, to provide some context," says Dr. Wibbelsman. "Find out what's in the movie, what's in the program, what's on that Internet site before you let your child see or hear. And experience with him or her together, so you can discuss it and use it to build trust between you."

Starting the Discussion

So when is the right time to start talking about sex with [a] child? It's a good idea to start laying the groundwork for these conversations long before the onset of puberty. The more frequently and frankly sexual matters are discussed, the easier and even more open such discussions are likely to be as you both grow comfortable with talking about it. "Let's face it, we're all embarrassed to talk about sex with each other," Dr. Seigel says. "The easiest way to start is to be real with your adolescent: 'This is really hard for me to talk about and it was hard for me to talk about with my dad when I was your age.' But it's important to talk about, and we have to talk about embarrassing things sometimes."

Keep reminding [the] child that you are in her corner every step of the way. "Never let them forget that your love is unconditional," Dr. Seigel says. "Tell them, 'I am here with you, and I love you and I will be here with you no matter what through all of this.' Yes, it's much easier said than done, but no less important."

So what should you talk about? Perhaps start with how sexuality is portrayed in the media and, far more importantly, how it "works" in real life—the potentially bad consequences and catastrophes than can be a result of sexual activity, as well as the pleasure and positive results of responsible sexuality (remember: the job here is to be honest.) "You see a character in a TV show who's made a decision with regard to sex," Dr. Seigel says. "Start the discussion there, but don't make it your soapbox. If you harshly criticize what you're both seeing, your child will assume there's no discussion to be had, and there goes your channel of communication."

By approaching the topic carefully and conversationally, [the parent and] child are much more likely to sort through the complexities together.

Keeping the Channels Open

As [the] child matures—physically, mentally, and emotionally—opportunities will emerge for making regular discussions about sexuality part of [the] continuing conversation. Obviously, changes in [a] child's body as puberty begins are crucial markers for such conversations.

One area that should receive particular attention is "urban myths"—bits of false information that "everyone" knows, passed along from adolescent to adolescent (and even from generation to generation: Don't be surprised to find that [a] child has heard some of the same myths and misinformation that circulated during your adolescence). Make clear, for instance, that oral sex is not without risks, that unprotected intercourse without ejaculation is not effective birth control, and so on. "It's very important to get the facts straight from the start, and share those facts with your child," says Dr. Wibbelsman. "That builds trust, and that trust is critical to guiding your adolescent through these challenging times."

In particular, be specific and accurate about the risks of pregnancy, the effectiveness (and limitations) of different types of birth control, and the variety of sexually transmitted diseases (STDs) and their effects.

Countering the Pressure

One key area to emphasize is that no one has the right to pressure [a child] to have sex. Peer pressure—and the media pressure that often stimulates it—can be addressed by empowering children with . . . belief in their ability to withstand such pressure, a sense of values that are more important than immediate gratification, and their absolute freedom to bring any concerns to [the parent].

It is wholly natural for adolescents to have questions about sex and sexual identity. While attitudes toward gay and lesbian identity (among other issues) remain tangled and complex, the crucial thing to bear in mind is that all of us have such questions at one time or another. "Parents need to be open about that and understand the entire spectrum of sexuality and sexual orientation, and not try to funnel them into a particular niche or area," says Dr. Wibbelsman. "Accept the adolescent's questions as part of growing up, because that's exactly what it is. But at the same time, let the adolescent know what your views and values are. Know the difference between facts and your opinion, and be clear about both."

But how to do it in a way that helps keep the channels open? It's a four-letter word, actually. "The key is to let adolescents know that you love them no matter who they become," Dr. Seigel says. "They may turn out tall, short, heavy, thin, healthy, or sickly—but you'll love them no matter what, no matter what decisions they make. That is much easier said than done for many parents, but that's key to raising a healthy adolescent."

And don't hesitate to discuss values, morals, and ethics with regard to sex—without lecturing, but with guidance. By providing [a] child with a solid framework of information and values, [parents have] taken a large step toward making sure that when he or she becomes sexually active it will be with the knowledge, preparation, and maturity that will mark the transition to sexual activity as an informed choice, not a risky accident.

Periodical and Internet Sources Bibliography

The following articles have been chosen to supplement the diverse views presented in this chapter.

Linda L. Barkacs and Craig B. Barkacs	"Do You Think I'm Sexty? Minors and Sexting: Teenage Fad or Child Pornography? *Journal of Legal, Ethical and Regulatory Issues*, November 2, 2010.
Benoit Denizet-Lewis	"It's Not U, It's Me," *New York Times Magazine*, August 7, 2011.
Sandy M. Fernandez	"A Young Girl's Sexting Trauma," *Redbook*, November 2011.
Jan Hoffman	"A Girl's Nude Photo, and Altered Lives," *New York Times*, March 26, 2011.
Laurie Penny	"There's More to the Facebook Generation than the Odd Poke," *New Statesman*, July 3, 2011.
Elizabeth M. Ryan	"Sexting: How the State Can Prevent a Moment of Indiscretion from Leading to a Lifetime of Unintended Consequences for Minors and Young Adults," *Iowa Law Review*, 2010.
Sandy Fertman Ryan	"The Real 'Reality' of Being a Teen Mom," *Girl's Life*, August–September 2011.
Natasha K. Segool and Tony D. Crespi	"Sexting in the Schoolyard," *Communiqué NASP* [National Association of School Psychologists], June 2011.
Somini Sengupta	"'Big Brother'? No. It's Parents," *New York Times*, June 25, 2012.
Kelly Beaucar Vlahos	"Born to Consume: For MTV, Teen Pregnancy Is Big Business," *American Conservative*, July 2011.
Washington Times	"Barely Legal: TV Peddles Teen Sex to Girls," December 21, 2010.

For Further Discussion

Chapter 1

1. Sadie F. Dingfelder argues that teen dating violence is a serious and hidden problem that many people dismiss. Mike Males claims, however, that activist organizations with their own agendas exaggerate to create a teen dating violence problem where none exists. What types of evidence does each author use to support his or her view? Which type of evidence do you think is more persuasive? Explain.

2. Rachel Aydt claims that one cause of teen dating violence is teens' lack of dating experience. Megan Twohey and Bonnie Miller Rubin assert that part of the teen dating violence problem is that many teens see dating violence as normal. Which cause do you think contributes most to teen dating violence? Did the authors' varying rhetorical styles influence your choice? Explain why or why not.

3. Ann Burke claims that, because anyone can be a victim, all students should learn to recognize the difference between unacceptable dating violence and healthy relationships. Heather Mac Donald asserts that the problem of teen dating violence is not universal, but due to other social problems. Does Burke's experience as the mother of a murdered dating violence victim make her evidence more or less persuasive? What are the risks of an emotional appeal? Does Mac Donald's distance from the teen dating violence problem make her more or less persuasive? What risks does Mac Donald take by basing her argument on assumptions about the values of those who support teen dating violence programs?

4. Identify the different rhetorical strategies the authors use to support their claims in this chapter. After noting the publications from which the viewpoints are excerpted and their primary readership, explain how the chosen rhetorical

strategy may vary depending on the audience for the authors' views.

Chapter 2

1. Bernadine Healy fears that many teens no longer take sex seriously and thus are unprepared for the risks and responsibilities of sex. Tara Parker-Pope believes, on the other hand, that unwarranted public fears about a teen casual sex epidemic are a reaction by parents to cultural changes. How does the occupation of each author reflect her rhetoric? Does this make one more persuasive? Explain why or why not.

2. Armstrong Williams believes that parents are in the best position to prevent their teens from having sex. Advocates for Youth argues that comprehensive sex education will best delay sex while also protecting those teens who do choose to have sex. Steve Martino asserts that for some teens, virginity pledges prevent the risks that accompany teen sex. What evidence do the authors provide to support their claims? How does this evidence influence the viewpoint's persuasiveness? Which strategy do you believe will be most effective to delay teen sex?

3. Marcia Kaye claims that the practice of dating in groups delays teen sex by reducing the risks that accompany more intimate dating relationships. Stephen G. Wallace argues that the lack of intimacy in the sexual practices of teens can lead to psychological problems. Both authors have a very different understanding of teen dating relationships. On what does Wallace base his view? On what does Kaye base her view? How does this influence their arguments?

4. Martha Kempner asserts that age-of-consent laws are so confusing and vary so much from state to state that laws designed to protect children from adult predators are actually hurting those the laws are designed to protect. Kempner

provides examples of various state laws. Which do you think best balances the need to protect children from predatory adults while avoiding absurd applications of the law that make criminals of teens having sex with their teen partners?

Chapter 3

1. Amanda Lenhart claims that sexting is a serious problem for many teens. Kaitlin Lounsbury, Kimberly J. Mitchell, and David Finkelhor argue that the studies that assert sexting is a serious problem for teens have limitations that affect their reliability. Their analysis discusses Lenhart's study prepared for the Pew Internet and American Life Project. Do you think these limitations make Lenhart's analysis less compelling? How might Lenhart answer Lounsbury, Mitchell, and Finkelhor's concerns? Explain, citing evidence from Lenhart's viewpoint.

2. Amanda Lenhart asserts that sexting is less common among teens whose parents limit their teen's texting and thus parents should consider setting limits. Break the Cycle claims, on the other hand, that teens often do not report problems they are having in dating relationships that involve technology as they fear parents will invade their privacy or limit their access to technology. Does either author suggest how parents can protect their teens without invading their teen's privacy or limiting their access to the benefits of technology? Explain.

3. Jane D. Brown, Sarah Keller, and Susannah Stern explore both the benefits and detriments of various media on teen sexual relationships. Which of these influences do you think has the most positive impact and which the most negative impact? Explain.

4. Katherine Suellentrop, Jane Brown, and Rebecca Ortiz assert that shows like MTV's *16 and Pregnant* can be useful educational tools to help teens understand the real risks

and rewards of teen pregnancy. Susie Kroll, however, claims that such shows glamorize teen pregnancy, tempting teens who have few options to choose pregnancy. Do you think parental monitoring or an adult-mediated discussion would overcome Kroll's concerns? Explain why or why not.

5. Bruce E. Pinkleton, Erica Weintraub Austin, Marilyn Cohen, Yi-Chun "Yvonnes" Chen, and Erin Fitzgerald argue that media literacy programs can effectively mediate the misleading media portrayals of teen dating relationships. Keith Ferrell feels that parents need to mediate the irresponsible messages about teens, relationships, and sex. The rhetoric of these two views varies significantly. How do the authors' affiliations and audiences influence these rhetorical choices?

6. Of the concerns on the impact of media and technology in the chapter, which do you think has the most significant impact on dating teens? Explain.

Organizations to Contact

The editors have compiled the following list of organizations concerned with the issues debated in this book. The descriptions are derived from materials provided by the organizations. All have publications or information available for interested readers. The list was compiled on the date of publication of the present volume; names, addresses, phone and fax numbers, and e-mail and Internet addresses may change. Be aware that many organizations take several weeks or longer to respond to inquiries, so allow as much time as possible.

Advocates for Youth
2000 M Street NW, Suite 750
Washington, DC 20036
(202) 419-3420 • fax: (202) 419-1448
website: www.advocatesforyouth.org

Advocates for Youth supports better and more effective sexual health and education programs and policies to prevent sexually transmitted diseases and reduce teen pregnancy. The organization supports youth access to condoms and contraception and sponsors media campaigns and public education programs to promote a more positive and realistic approach to adolescent sexual health. The organization envisions a society that views sexuality as normal and healthy and treats young people as a valuable resource. On its website Advocates for Youth provides access to articles on a broad range of youth sexuality issues, including abstinence, sex education, television and the Internet, and violence and harassment.

Break the Cycle
5777 W. Century Blvd., Suite 1150
Los Angeles, CA 90045
(310) 286-3383 • fax: (310) 286-3386

website: www.breakthecycle.org

Break the Cycle believes that teen dating violence is an epidemic. Thus, the organization works to engage, educate, and empower youth to build lives and communities free from dating violence. It provides tools for public education, training, and advocacy. On its Dating Violence 101 link, the organization provides facts and statistics on dating violence and state-by-state report cards on each state's legal responsiveness to the unique needs of teens.

Center for Media Literacy (CML)

23852 Pacific Coast Hwy., #472
Malibu, CA 90265
(310) 456-1225 • fax: (310) 456-0020
e-mail: cml@medialit.org
website: www.medialit.org

CML is a public education and professional development organization. The center works nationally, especially with the young, to help people develop critical thinking and media production skills. Its books can be purchased online, and the website offers free background information and articles about research on sex in the media, including "Sex on TV: Do All Kids See the Same Show?" and "Turning the Tables on TV Sex."

Center on Media and Child Health (CMCH)

300 Longwood Ave.
Boston, MA 01151
(617) 355-2000
e-mail: cmch@childrens.harvard.edu
website: www.cmch.tv

Based at Children's Hospital Boston, Harvard Medical School, and Harvard School of Public Health, CMCH conducts and compiles research that improves the understanding of the ways in which media affect children in positive and negative ways. It lends its expertise to programs that address children's exposure to the media. Current news articles, the CMCH blog, and a research engine are available on the organization's website.

The Coalition for Positive Sexuality (CPS)

PO Box 77212
Washington, DC 20013
(773) 604-1654
website: www.positive.org

In 1996 CPS began as a poster project geared toward girls that encouraged them to acknowledge their sexuality, not deny it. Today it offers useful information about safe sex and sexually transmitted diseases. Its current publication *Just Say Yes* can be obtained by visiting the website.

Media Awareness Network (MNet)

1500 Merivale Road, 3rd Floor
Ottowa, Ontario, Canada K2E 6Z5
(613) 224-7721
e-mail: info@media-awareness.ca
website: www.media-awareness.ca

MNet is a team of educators, journalists, and people with backgrounds in mass communication and cultural policy. Its goal is to provide youth with knowledge about how the media work and how media affect them and the choices they make. The website offers separate resources for teachers and parents as well as a blog and news on current issues regarding the media.

National Abstinence Education Association (NAEA)

1701 Pennsylvania Ave. NW, Suite 300
Washington, DC 10006
(202) 248-5420 • fax: (866) 935-4850
e-mail: info@theNAEA.org
website: www.abstinenceassociation.org

NAEA promotes abstinence education through lobbying and public information. The association publishes a free newsletter, past issues of which are available on its website. Also available on its website are articles on abstinence education research, including "Let's Talk About Sex" and "More Happiness for Couples Who Wait."

The National Campaign to Prevent Teen and Unplanned Pregnancy

1776 Massachusetts Ave. NW, Suite 200
Washington, DC 20036
(202) 478-8500 • fax: (202) 478-8588
website: www.thenationalcampaign.org

The National Campaign to Prevent Teen and Unplanned Pregnancy was formed in 1996 with the objective to decrease teen pregnancy in America. By working with policy makers, the media, and state and local leaders, the organization provides the materials it believes are needed to educate various audiences on the prevention of teen pregnancy. On its Special Focus link, the group provides portals to address specific issues and groups such as males, parents, policy makers, and teens. Its Resources link contains articles on teens, including "The Cautious Generation? Teens Tell Us About Sex, Virginity, and 'The Talk,'" "Kiss and Tell: What Teens Say About Love, Trust, and Other Relationship Stuff," and "Freeze Frame 2012: A Snapshot of America's Teens."

National Center for Missing and Exploited Children (NCMEC)

699 Prince Street
Alexandria, VA 22314
(800) THE-LOST; (703) 739-0321 • fax: (703) 224-1212
website: www.missingkids.com

NCMEC works with law enforcement and serves as a clearinghouse of information on the problem of missing and exploited children. While its focus is on crimes against children, the center also provides information on Internet safety and publishes fact sheets and a policy statement on sexting, which are available on its website.

Planned Parenthood Federation of America

434 West 33rd Street
New York, NY 10001
(212) 541-7800 • fax: (212) 245-1845
website: www.plannedparenthood.org

For over ninety years Planned Parenthood has provided information to young women to help them make informed decisions regarding health, sex, and family planning. It has more than 840 health centers nationwide that offer safe, quality health care, 90 percent of which is preventive and primary care. It also has begun to expand globally, placing centers in Africa, Asia, and throughout Latin America. Readers can search the website for information on many health topics.

Sexuality Information and Education Council of the United States (SIECUS)

130 West 42nd Street, Suite 350
New York, NY 10036
(212) 819-9770
e-mail: pmalone@siecus.org
website: www.siecus.org

SIECUS provides a place where sexuality is viewed as natural and healthy. Since it began, the organization has taken a stand on major issues concerning sexuality, including the role of sexuality in society and culture. SIECUS was founded in 1964 with the goal of providing education and information regarding sexuality and sexual and reproductive health. It views sexuality as a part of being human and works to protect social justice and the sexual rights of everyone. The website provides information about the different sex education programs as well as links to several publications, which are available for download at no cost.

US Department of Justice Office on Violence Against Women (OVW)

800 K Street NW, Suite 920
Washington, DC 20530
(202) 307-6026 • fax: (202) 305-2589
website: www.ovw.usdoj.gov

The OVW provides federal leadership to reduce violence against women, dating violence, sexual assault, and stalking. The office also administers Violence Against Women Act grants to state, local, tribal, and nonprofit entities that respond to violence against women. The OVW website publishes fact sheets on teen dating violence. Other OVW publications on teen dating violence can be found at the National Criminal Justice Reference Service website (www.ncjrs.gov).

Bibliography of Books

Louisa Allen

Young People and Sexuality Education: Rethinking Key Debates. New York: Palgrave Macmillan, 2011.

Judith K. Balswick and Jack O. Balswick

Authentic Human Sexuality: An Integrated Christian Approach. Downers Grove, IL: InterVarsity Press, 2008.

Sideris Bastas

Teens and Technology: What Makes Your Teen Tick and How to Keep Them Safe. Frederick, MD: Publish America, 2000.

Kathy Belge and Mark Bieschke

Queer: The Ultimate LGBT Guide for Teens. San Francisco: Zest Books, 2011.

Dennis Carlson and Donyell Roseboro, eds.

The Sexuality Curriculum and Youth Culture. New York: Peter Lang, 2011.

Heather Corinna

S.E.X.: The All-You-Need-to-Know Progressive Sexuality Guide to Get You Through High School and College. New York: Marlowe, 2007.

Alesha E. Doan and Jean Calterone Williams

The Politics of Virginity: Abstinence in Sex Education. New York: Praeger, 2008.

M. Gigi Durham

The Lolita Effect: The Media Sexualization of Young Girls and What We Can Do About It. Woodstock, NY: Overlook Press, 2009.

Chad Eastham, Bill Farrel, and Pam Farrel	*Guys Are Waffles, Girls Are Spaghetti.* Nashville: Thomas Nelson, 2009.
Naomi B. Farber	*Adolescent Pregnancy: Policy and Prevention Services.* New York: Springer, 2009.
Heather Godsey and Lara Blackwood Pickrel, eds.	*Oh God, Oh God, Oh God! Young Adults Speak Out About Sexuality and Christian Spirituality.* St. Louis: Chalice Press, 2010.
Miriam Grossman	*You're Teaching My Child What? A Physician Exposes the Lies of Sex Education and How They Harm Your Child.* Washington, DC: Regnery, 2009.
Nikol Hasler	*Sex: A Book for Teens.* San Francisco: Zest Books, 2010.
Kelly Huegel	*GLBTQ: The Survival Guide for Gay, Lesbian, Bisexual, Transgender, and Questioning Teens.* Minneapolis: Free Spirit, 2011.
Brenda Hunter and Kristen Blair	*From Santa to Sexting.* Abilene, TX: Abilene Christian University, 2012.
Diane E. Levin and Jean Kilbourne	*So Sexy So Soon: The New Sexualized Childhood and What Parents Can Do to Protect Their Kids.* New York: Ballantine Books, 2008.
Barry Levy	*In Love and In Danger: A Teen's Guide to Breaking Free of Abusive Relationships.* Berkeley: Seal Press, 2006.

Mike A. Males — *Teenage Sex and Pregnancy: Modern Myths, Unsexy Realities.* Santa Barbara, CA: Praeger/ABC-CLIO, 2010.

Sharon Maxwell — *The Talk: A Breakthrough Guide to Raising Healthy Kids in an Oversexualized, Online, In-Your-Face World.* New York: Penguin, 2008.

Joe S. McIlhaney and Freda McKissic Bush — *Hooked: New Science on How Casual Sex Is Affecting Our Children.* Chicago: Northfield, 2008.

Jill A. Murray — *But He Never Hit Me: The Devastating Cost of Non-Physical Abuse to Girls and Women.* Bloomington, IN: iUniverse, 2007.

Amy Schalet — *Not Under My Roof: Parents, Teens, and the Culture of Sex.* Chicago: University of Chicago Press, 2011.

Jessica Valenti — *The Purity Myth: How America's Obsession with Virginity Is Hurting Young Women.* Berkeley: Seal Press, 2010.

Elin Stebbins Waldal — *Tornado Warning: A Memoir of Teen Dating Violence and Its Effect on a Woman's Life.* Encinitas, CA: Sound Beach, 2011.

Valerie Wee — *Teen Media: Hollywood and the Youth Market in the Digital Age.* Jefferson, NC: McFarland and Co., 2010.

Index

CPSIA information can be obtained
at www.ICGtesting.com
Printed in the USA
FFOW030813280213

9 780737 763454